My
Facebook®
for Seniors

SECOND EDITION

Michael Miller

800 East 96th Street,
Indianapolis, Indiana 46240 USA

Real Possibilities

My Facebook® for Seniors, Second Edition

Copyright © 2015 by Pearson Education, Inc.

ISBN-13: 978-0-7897-5431-8
ISBN-10: 0-7897-5431-2

Library of Congress Control Number: 2014952958

Printed in the United States of America

First Printing: December 2014

Trademarks

Warning and Disclaimer

Special Sales

For information about buying this title in bulk quantities, or for special sales opportunities (which may include electronic versions; custom cover designs; and content particular to your business, training goals, marketing focus, or branding interests), please contact our corporate sales department at corpsales@pearsoned.com or (800) 382-3419.

For government sales inquiries, please contact governmentsales@pearsoned.com.

For questions about sales outside the U.S., please contact international@pearsoned.com.

Editor-in-Chief
Greg Wiegand

Acquisitions Editor
Michelle Newcomb

Marketing
Dan Powell

Director, AARP Books
Jodi Lipson

**Development/
Copy Editor**
Charlotte Kughen,
The Wordsmithery LLC

Managing Editor
Kristy Hart

Senior Project Editor
Lori Lyons

Indexer
Cheryl Lenser

Proofreader
Debbie Williams

Technical Editor
Vince Averello

Editorial Assistant
Cindy Teeters

Cover Designer
Mark Shirar

Compositor
Kim Scott, Bumpy Design

Contents at a Glance

Table of Contents

14   Attending Events and Celebrating Birthdays   189

15   Playing Games   203

About the Author

Michael Miller is a prolific and popular writer of more than 150 non-fiction books, known for his ability to explain complex topics to everyday readers. He writes about a variety of topics, including technology, business, and music. His best-selling books for Que include *My Windows 8.1 Computer for Seniors, Facebook for Grown-Ups, Easy Facebook, Easy Computer Basics, Computer Basics: Absolute Beginner's Guide,* and *My Pinterest.* Worldwide, his books have sold more than 1 million copies.

Find out more at the author's website: www.millerwriter.com

Follow the author on Twitter: molehillgroup

Dedication

To my grandkids, who make my life fun and meaningful—Collin, Alethia, Hayley, Judah, and Lacl.

Acknowledgments

Thanks to all the folks at Que who helped turned this manuscript into a book, including Michelle Newcomb, Greg Wiegand, Charlotte Kughen, Lori Lyons, Kim Scott, and technical editor Vince Averello. Thanks also to the kind folks at AARP for adding even more to the project.

About AARP and AARP TEK

AARP is a nonprofit, nonpartisan organization, with a membership of nearly 38 million, that helps people turn their goals and dreams into *real possibilities*™, strengthens communities, and fights for the issues that matter most to families such as healthcare, employment and income security, retirement planning, affordable utilities, and protection from financial abuse. Learn more at aarp.org.

The AARP TEK (Technology Education & Knowledge) program aims to accelerate AARP's mission of turning dreams into *real possibilities*™ by providing step-by-step lessons in a variety of formats to accommodate different learning styles, levels of experience, and interests. Expertly guided hands-on workshops delivered in communities nationwide help instill confidence and enrich lives of the 50+ by equipping them with skills for staying connected to the people and passions in their lives. Lessons are taught on touchscreen tablets and smartphones—common tools for connection, education, entertainment, and productivity. For self-paced lessons, videos, articles, and other resources, visit aarptek.org.

Note: Most of the individuals pictured throughout this book are of the author himself, as well as friends and relatives (and sometimes pets). Some names and personal information are fictitious.

We Want to Hear from You!

As the reader of this book, you are our most important critic and commentator. We value your opinion and want to know what we're doing right, what we could do better, what areas you'd like to see us publish in, and any other words of wisdom you're willing to pass our way.

We welcome your comments. You can email or write to let us know what you did or didn't like about this book—as well as what we can do to make our books better.

Please note that we cannot help you with technical problems related to the topic of this book.

When you write, please be sure to include this book's title and author as well as your name and email address. We will carefully review your comments and share them with the author and editors who worked on the book.

Email: feedback@quepublishing.com

Mail: Que Publishing
          ATTN: Reader Feedback
          800 East 96th Street
          Indianapolis, IN 46240 USA

Reader Services

Visit our website and register this book at www.quepublishing.com/register for convenient access to any updates, downloads, or errata that might be available for this book.

Sign in to your current
Facebook account.

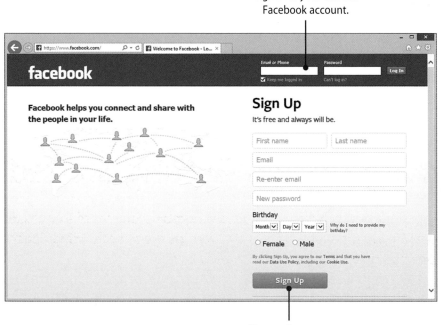

Sign up for a new
Facebook account.

In this chapter, you find out how to create a new Facebook account and start using the Facebook site.

Signing Up and Getting Started

Facebook has more than one billion members online, of all ages and types. Chances are your family and friends are already using Facebook—which means it's time for you to join in, too.

Understanding Social Networking

Facebook is a *social network*. This is a large website that hosts a community of users, which makes it easy for those users to communicate with one another. Social networks enable users to share experiences and opinions with one another, and thus keep in touch with friends and family members, no matter where they're located.

The goal of a social network is to create a network of online "friends," and then share your activities with them via a series of message posts. These posts are short text messages, called *status updates,* which can be viewed by all your friends on the site. A status update can be text only, or contain photos, videos, and links to other web pages.

Your online friends read your posts, as well as posts from other friends, in a continuously updated stream. On Facebook, this stream is called the *News Feed*, and it's the one place where you can read updates from all your online friends and family; it's where you find out what's really happening.

There are many social networks on the Internet, and Facebook is the largest. (Other popular social networks include Twitter, LinkedIn, Google+, and Pinterest.) With more than one billion users worldwide, chances are many of your friends and family are already using Facebook.

Facebook was launched by Mark Zuckerberg while he was a student at Harvard in 2004. Facebook (originally called "thefacebook") was originally intended as a site where college students could socialize online. Sensing opportunity beyond the college market, Facebook opened its site to high school students in 2005, and then to all users over age 13 in 2006.

Although Facebook started as a network for college students, today it's the social network of choice for users of all ages. In fact, half of all people aged 65 or older who are online make Facebook their hub for online social activity—and browse the site for at least an hour each day.

Signing Up for Facebook

When you're signed up as a Facebook member, you can post your own thoughts and comments, upload pictures to share, and even share your favorite web pages. Likewise, you can see what your friends and family are posting—their activities, photos, web links, and the like.

Create a New Facebook Account

To use Facebook, you first need to create a personal Facebook account. A Facebook account is free and easy to create; there's no fee to join and no monthly membership fees.

(1) Use Firefox, Google Chrome, Internet Explorer, Safari, or another web browser to go to Facebook's home page at www.facebook.com.

(2) Go to the Sign Up section and enter your first name into the First Name box.

(3) Enter your last name into the Last Name box.

(4) Enter your email address into the Email box and then re-enter it into the Re-enter Email box.

Email Address

Facebook uses your email address to confirm your identity and to contact you when necessary. You also use your email address to sign into Facebook each time you enter the site.

(5) Enter your desired password into the New Password box. Your password should be at least six characters in length—the longer the better, for security reasons.

facebook

Sign Up

It's free and always will be.

First name   Last name

Email

Re-enter email

New password

Birthday

Month ☑ Day ☑ Year ☑   Why do I need to provide my birthday?

○ Female   ○ Male

By clicking Sign Up, you agree to our **Terms** and that you have read our **Data Use Policy**, including our **Cookie Use**.

Sign Up

>>>Go Further
PASSWORD SECURITY

To make your password harder for hackers to guess, include a mix of alphabetic (upper- and lowercase), numeric, and special characters, such as punctuation marks. You can also make your password more secure by making it longer; an eight-character password is much harder to crack than a six-character one. Just remember, though, that the more complex you make your password, the more difficult it may be for you to remember—which means you probably need to write it down somewhere, just in case. (Just make sure wherever you write it down is kept well-hidden and secure!)

(6) Select your date of birth from the Birthday list. (You can later choose to hide this information if you want; see Chapter 19, "Managing Your Facebook Account," to learn how.)

(7) Check the appropriate option for your gender.

(8) Click the Sign Up button.

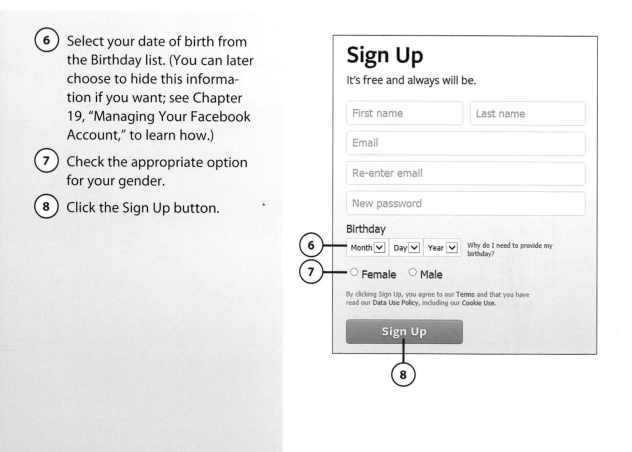

9 Facebook wants to know if any of your real-world friends are on Facebook, and whether you want to add them to your list of Facebook friends. You can do this now or do this later; if you want to find friends from among your email contacts, click the Find Friends button and follow the onscreen instructions.

10 Facebook prompts you to enter information for your profile. You can do this now or do this later (by clicking Skip). To enter this information now, enter the city where you currently live, your hometown, high school, college or university attended, and current employer. Note that this information is optional; if you enter it, however, it will be easier to find people you know on Facebook. Click Next when ready.

11 Facebook prompts you to add a profile picture. You can do this now or do this later (by clicking Skip). To upload a picture from your computer, click Add Picture and locate the picture you want. To take a new picture with your computer's webcam, click Take a Photo and, when ready, click the Take button. Click Next when ready.

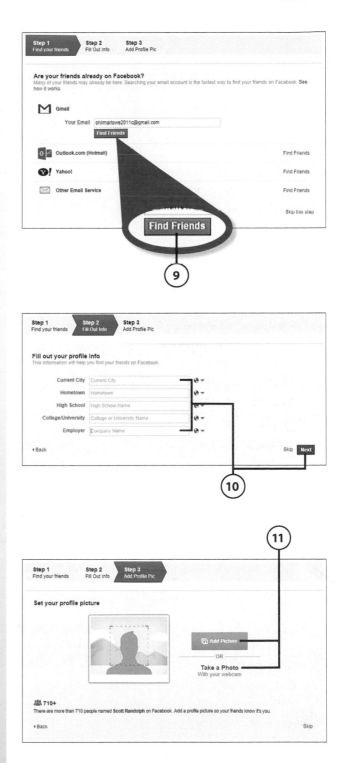

(12) Facebook now displays a Welcome screen. Click News Feed in the left side menu to view your Facebook News Feed and begin using Facebook.

CAPTCHA

When Facebook displays the Security Check page, you're prompted to enter the "secret words" from the CAPTCHA into the Text in the Box box. A CAPTCHA is a type of challenge-response test to ensure that you're actually a human being rather than a computer program. Websites use CAPTCHAs to cut down on the amount of computer-generated spam they receive.

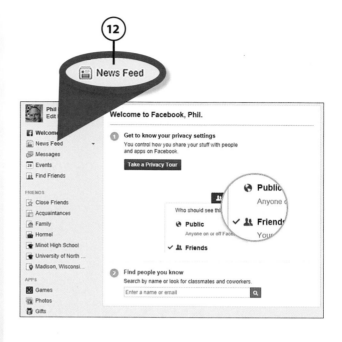

>>>Go Further
EMAIL CONFIRMATION AND MORE

After you click the final Sign Up button, Facebook sends you an email message asking you to confirm your new Facebook account. When you receive this email, click the link to proceed.

You'll then be prompted to find friends who are already on Facebook, and to fill in a few personal details for your profile page. You can perform these tasks now or at a later time, as we'll discuss later in this book.

Signing In—and Signing Out

After you've created your Facebook account, you can sign into the site and start finding new (and old) friends. You sign in at the same page you created your account—www.facebook.com.

Log On to the Facebook Site

You use your email address—and the password you created during the signup process—to log in to your Facebook account. When you're logged in, Facebook displays your home page.

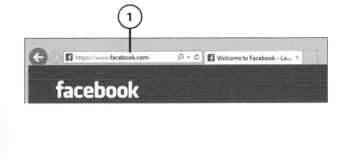

(1) Use Firefox, Google Chrome, Internet Explorer, Safari, or another web browser to go to Facebook's home page at www.facebook.com.

(2) Enter your email address into the Email or Phone box.

(3) Enter your password into the Password box.

(4) Click the Log In button.

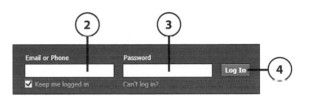

>>>Go Further
STAY LOGGED IN—OR NOT

If you don't want to enter your email and password every time you want to use the Facebook site, check the Keep Me Logged In option when you're signing in. This keeps your Facebook session open, even if you visit another website between Facebook pages.

You should not check the Keep Me Logged In option if you're using a public computer, such as one at the library, or if you share your computer with other users. Doing so makes it possible for other users to use your personal Facebook account, which you don't want. If you share your computer or use a public computer, don't check the Keep Me Logged In option.

Log Out of Your Facebook Account

You probably want to log out of Facebook if you're not going to be active for an extended period of time. You also want to log out if someone else in your household wants to access his or her Facebook account.

(1) From any Facebook page, click the down arrow button at the far right side of the toolbar.

(2) Click Log Out from the drop-down menu.

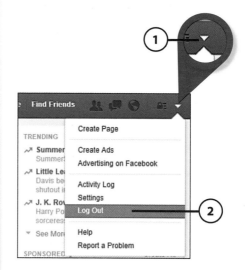

Sign Back In

After you've logged out, you need to sign back in before you can access your Facebook content again.

Finding Your Way Around Facebook

You discover more about using Facebook throughout the balance of this book, but for now let's examine how to get around the Facebook site. When it comes to moving from place to place on Facebook, you have two choices. You can use either the Facebook toolbar that appears at the top of every page, or the navigation pane that's displayed on the left side of all pages. Not all options are found in both places.

Navigate Facebook's Home Page

After you sign into your Facebook account, you see Facebook's home page. This page looks a little different for each user, as it displays content personalized for you.

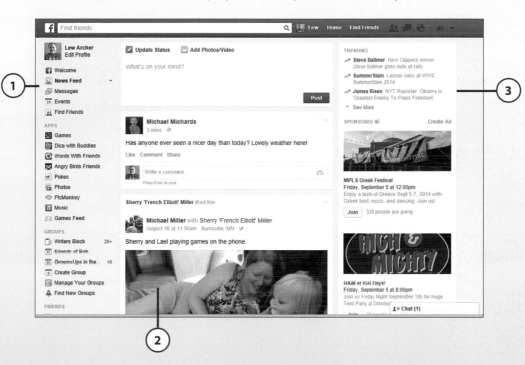

1. On the left side of the page is the *navigation sidebar*, or what Facebook imaginatively calls the *left side menu*. You use the options here to go to various places on the Facebook site.

2. The large column in the middle of the home page displays your *News Feed*, a stream of posts from all your Facebook friends. At the top of this column is a box you use to post your own status updates.

3. The column on the right side of the page displays various Facebook notices and advertisements.

Use the Facebook Toolbar

The toolbar that appears at the top of every Facebook page is your primary means of navigating the Facebook site. The toolbar also provides notification when you have messages waiting or if a friend engages you in a specific activity.

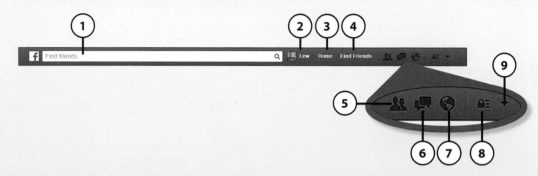

(1)   Search the Facebook site for people or things by entering your query into the Search box; click the search (magnifying glass) icon or press Enter on your computer keyboard to start the search.

(2)   Click your name to view your own personal timeline page.

(3)   Click the Home button at any time to return to the Home page.

(4)   If your toolbar displays the Find Friends button (it probably will if you're new), click it to view suggested people for your Facebook friends list.

(5)   Click the Friend Requests button to view any friend requests you've received and to search for new friends on the Facebook site.

(6)   Click the Messages button to view your most recent private messages from Facebook friends.

(7)   Click the Notifications button to view notifications from Facebook, such as someone commenting on your status or accepting your friend request.

(8)   Click the lock icon to access important privacy settings. Read more about privacy settings in Chapter 18, "Managing Your Privacy on Facebook."

(9)   Click the down arrow button at the far right to access all sorts of account settings. This is also where you sign out of Facebook when you're done using it for the day.

Counting Requests and Messages

If you have pending friend requests, you see a white number in a red box on top of the Friend Requests button. (The number indicates how many requests you have.) Similarly, a white number in a red box on top of the Messages or Notifications buttons indicates how many unread messages or notifications you have.

Navigate with the Left Side Menu

You can get to even more features on Facebook when you use the navigation sidebar on the left side of the screen. Click any item to display that specific page.

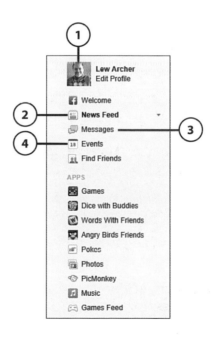

(1) To visit your personal timeline page, click your picture at the top of the menu. To edit your profile that appears on the timeline page, click Edit Profile.

(2) To read posts from your Facebook friends, click News Feed. To switch your News Feed from the default Top Stories display to instead display your friends' most recent posts, click the down arrow next to News Feed and click Most Recent.

(3) To view messages in your Facebook inbox, or send a private message to another user, click Messages.

(4) To view pending events or schedule a new event, click Events.

5 Any Facebook apps or games you use are listed in the Apps section. Click the name of a game or app to launch it.

6 Any Facebook interest groups you've subscribed to are listed in the Groups section. Click the name of a group to view that group's Facebook page.

7 Facebook lets you organize your friends into friends groups (not to be confused with interest groups), which are listed in the Friends section. Click the name of a friends group to view all posts from friends in that group.

Use the Right Side Menu

The column on the right side of Facebook's Home page contains some items you might find useful, and some you might not.

(1) The top of the column displays any events you've been invited to, as well as any friends who have upcoming birthdays.

(2) The Trending section displays the hottest topics at this moment on Facebook. Click a topic to read posts related to that topic.

(3) Beneath the Trending section is a section that sometimes displays suggested groups or friends, and almost always a section of ads ("sponsored" posts). Ignore these as you like.

(4) At the bottom-right corner of the Facebook window is the Chat bar. Click this to display a Chat list of friends who are currently online and free to chat. Click a name to initiate a chat session with that person.

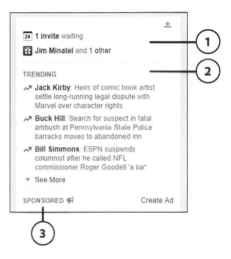

Widescreen Displays

If your computer display (and browser window) is wide enough, Facebook actually displays *four* columns. The fourth column displays the Ticker and Chat list whereas the third column now displays only ads and suggestions.

Check out friend requests.

Search for friends from your email contacts.

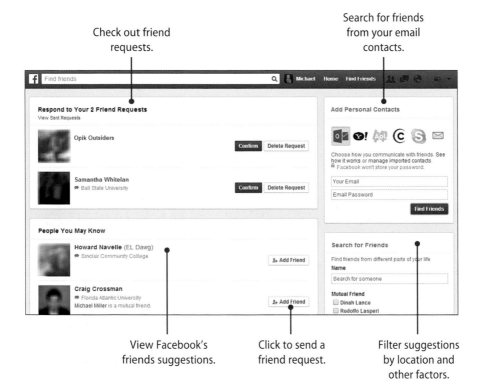

View Facebook's friends suggestions.

Click to send a friend request.

Filter suggestions by location and other factors.

In this chapter, you find out how to find people you know on Facebook and add them to your friends list.

→ Finding Facebook Friends
→ Accepting Friend Requests
→ Unfriending Unwanted Friends

2

Finding Old (and New) Friends on Facebook

Facebook is all about connecting with people you know. Anyone you connect with on Facebook is called a *friend*. A Facebook friend can be a real friend, or a family member, colleague, acquaintance… you name it. When you add people to your Facebook friends list, they see everything you post—and you see everything they post.

Of course, before you can make someone your Facebook friend, you have to find that person on Facebook. That isn't always as easy as you might think, especially when you're looking for people you went to school with or worked with several decades ago. People move, women might change their names when they get married (or divorced, or remarried, or some combination of the above), and it just becomes more difficult to find people over time. It might be difficult, but if they're on Facebook, you can probably find them.

Finding Facebook Friends

Because it's in Facebook's best interests for you to have as many connections as possible, the site makes it easy for you to find potential friends. This process is made easier by the fact that Facebook already knows a lot about you, based on the information you entered when you first signed up.

Facebook automatically suggests friends based on your personal history (where you've lived, worked, or gone to school), mutual friends (friends of people you're already friends with), and Facebook users who are in your email contacts lists. You can then invite any of these people to be your friend; if they accept, they're added to your Facebook friends list.

Facebook Friends

As far as Facebook is concerned, everyone you know is a "friend"—even family members. So when we talk about Facebook friends, these could be your brothers and sisters, children or grandchildren, neighbors, people you work with, casual acquaintances, or even real friends.

Accept Facebook's Friend Suggestions

The easiest way to find friends on Facebook is to let Facebook find them for you based on the information you provided for your personal profile. The more Facebook knows about you, especially in terms of where you've lived, worked, and gone to school, the more friends it can find.

How Many Friends?

Some people like to assemble a large list of Facebook friends, to keep in touch with everyone they've known throughout their lives. Other people find a large friends list somewhat overwhelming, and prefer to keep a shorter list of close friends and family.

Either approach is good. It all depends on what you want to get out of Facebook, and what you're comfortable with. Don't feel obligated to accept every friend suggestion or request; add to your list only those people you really, truly want to keep in contact with.

(**1**) If you have a Find Friends button on the Facebook toolbar, click it. Otherwise, click the Friends button to display the drop-down menu, and then click Find Friends.

(**2**) This displays a page that lists any friend requests you've received and offers a number of friend suggestions from Facebook in the People You May Know section. Keep scrolling down the page to view more friend suggestions.

Suggested Friends

The people Facebook suggests as friends are typically people who went to the same schools you did, worked at the same companies you did, or are friends of your current friends.

(**3**) To send a request for that person to be a friend, click the Add Friend button next to that person's name.

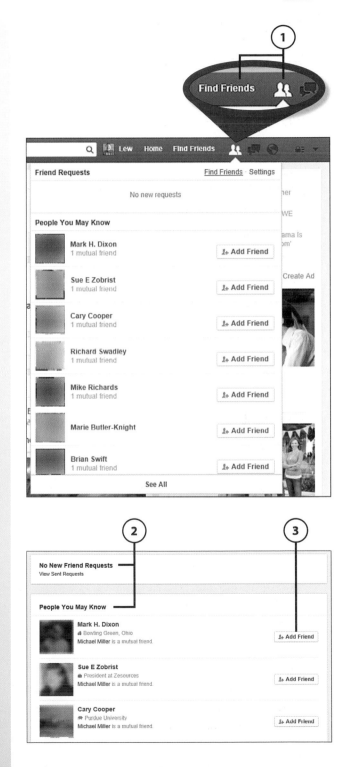

4 In the right column of the page, scroll down until you see the Search for Friends panel. To search for someone by name, enter that person's name into the Name box.

5 To search for people who are already friends with your other Facebook friends, go to the Mutual Friend section and check the names of one or more friends. (If a particular friend isn't listed, enter his or her name into the text box first.)

6 To look for people who come from your hometown, go to the Hometown section and check your town. (If your hometown isn't listed, enter it into the text box first.)

7 To search for people who live near you now, go to the Current City section and check your city. (If your town or city isn't listed, enter it into the text box first.)

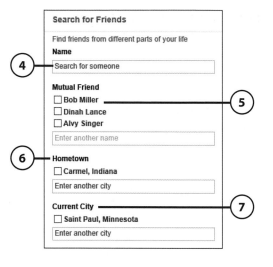

8 To search for people who went to the same high school you did, go to the High School section and check the name of your high school. (If your high school isn't listed, enter it into the text box first.)

9 To search for people who went to the same college or university you did, go to the College or University section and check the name of your school. (If your school isn't listed, enter its name into the text box first.)

10 To search for people who work or worked at one of your current or former employers, go to the Employer section and check the name of that company. (If a company isn't listed, enter its name into the text box first.)

11 To search for former classmates who went to the same graduate school you did (if, in fact, you went to graduate school), go to the Graduate School section and check the name of that school. (If your grad school isn't listed, enter its name into the text box first.)

12 Whichever options you select, Facebook returns a list of suggested friends based on your selection. Click the Add Friend button to send a friend request to a specific person.

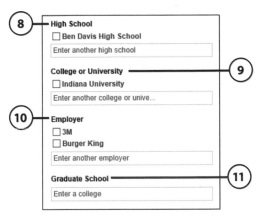

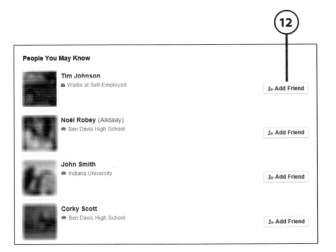

>>>Go Further
INVITATIONS

When you click the Add Friend button, Facebook doesn't automatically add that person to your friends list. Instead, that person receives an invitation to be your friend; she can accept or reject the invitation. If a person accepts your request, you become friends with that person. If a person does not accept your request, you don't become friends. (You are not notified if your friend request is declined.) In other words, you both have to agree to be friends—it's not a one-sided thing.

Find Email Contacts

Another way to find Facebook friends is to let Facebook look through your email contact lists for people who are also Facebook members. You can then invite those people to be your friends.

>>>Go Further
CONTACT SEARCHING

Facebook can search contacts from a variety of web-based email and communications services, including AOL, Gmail, iCloud, Outlook.com/Windows Live Hotmail, Skype, and Yahoo! Mail.

This process works by matching the email addresses in your contact lists with the email addresses users provide as their Facebook login. When Facebook finds a match, it suggests that person as a potential friend.

Finding Email Contacts

(1) If you have a Find Friends button on the Facebook toolbar, click it. Otherwise, click the Friends button to display the drop-down menu, then click Find Friends.

(2) On the top right side of the Friends page you see the Add Personal Contacts panel. Click the logo for the email service or contacts application you use.

(3) Enter your email address and password, as requested.

(4) Click the Find Friends button.

Sign In

At this point you might be prompted to sign into your email account or to link your email and Facebook accounts. Enter the required information to proceed.

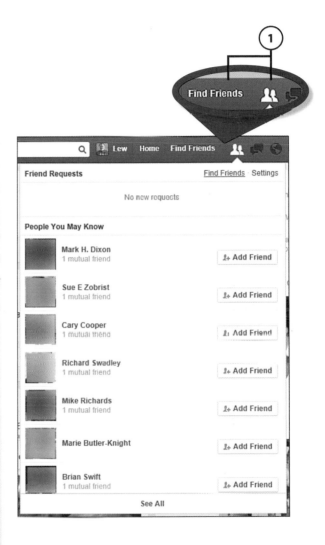

5) Facebook displays a list of your email contacts who are also Facebook members. Check the box next to each person with whom you'd like to be friends.

6) Click the Add Friends button to send friend requests to these contacts, or click Skip to go to the next step.

7) You see a list of your other friends who are not yet Facebook members. Check the box next to each person you'd like to become a Facebook member (and join your friends list).

8) Click the Send Invites button.

Search for Old Friends

If Facebook doesn't automatically suggest a particular friend, there's still a good chance that person is already on Facebook and waiting for you to find him. It's your task to find that person—by searching the Facebook site.

1) Start to type a person's name into the search box at the top of any Facebook page. As you type, Facebook displays a list of suggestions.

2) If your friend is listed, click the person's name to go to his Timeline page.

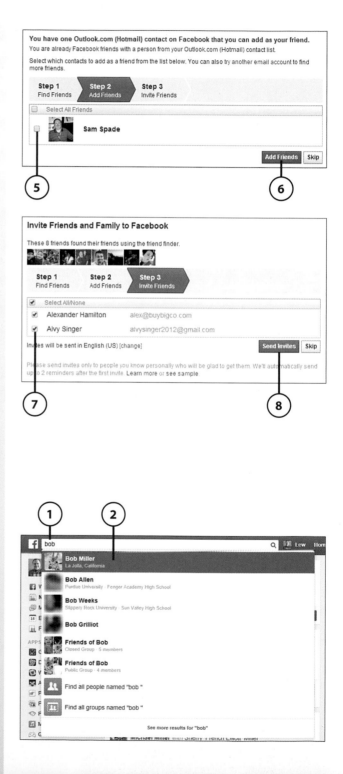

3 Click the Add Friend button to send an invitation to this person.

4 If the person was not listed in the search suggestions, click Find All People Named to display a list of people with that name. (You might need to click the See More link to display this option.)

5 You can filter this list to display people who live in a specific location, work or have worked at a given company, have attended a specific school, and so forth. Go to the filter box on the right side of the page, click the Add button for the filter you'd like to apply, and then select an item from the list.

6 Click the Add Friend button to send a friend request.

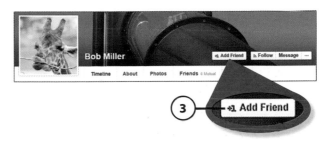

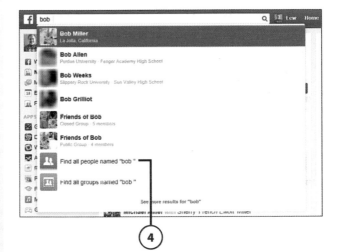

>>>Go Further

FINDING HARD-TO-FIND FRIENDS

When it comes to tracking down old friends on Facebook, sometimes a little detective work is in order. It's especially tough to find women you used to know, as names sometimes are changed along with marital status. Some women have enough forethought to enter their maiden name as their middle name on Facebook, so the Cathy Coolidge you used to know might be listed as Cathy Coolidge Smith, which means her maiden name actually shows up in a Facebook search. Others, however, don't do this—and thus become harder to find.

You can, of course, search for a partial name—searching just for "Cathy," for example. What happens next is a little interesting. Facebook returns a list of people named Cathy, of course, but puts at the top of this list people who have mutual friends in common with you. That's a nice touch, as it's likely that your old friend has already made a connection with another one of your Facebook friends.

Past that point, you can then display everyone on Facebook with that single name. But that's going to be a bit unwieldy, unless your friend has a unique name.

One approach to narrowing down the results is to filter your search results by location. For example, if you're looking for a John Smith and think he currently lives in Minnesota, use the Search Tools section at the top of the search results page to display only people who live in Minnesota. You can also filter by school (Education) and employer (Workplace).

Beyond these tips, finding long-lost friends on Facebook is a trial-and-error process. The best advice is to keep plugging—if they're on Facebook, you'll likely find them sooner or later.

Look for Friends of Friends

Another way to find old friends is to look for people who are friends of your current friends. That is, when you make someone your friend on Facebook, you can browse through the list of people who are on his friends list. Chances are you'll find mutual friends on this list—people that both of you know but you haven't found otherwise.

1. Click your friend's name anywhere on the Facebook site, such as in a status update, to display his Timeline page.

2. Click Friends under the person's name to display his Friends page, which lists all of this person's Facebook friends.

3. When you find a person you'd like to be friends with, click the Add Friend button.

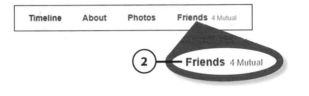

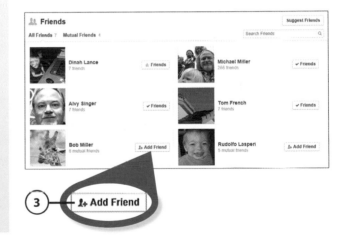

Accepting Friend Requests

Sometimes potential Facebook friends find you before you find them. When this happens, they will send you a friend request, which you can then accept or decline. You might receive a friend request via email, or you can view friend requests within Facebook.

Accept a Friend Request

You can also access all your pending friend requests from the Facebook toolbar—and then decide whether to accept or decline the request.

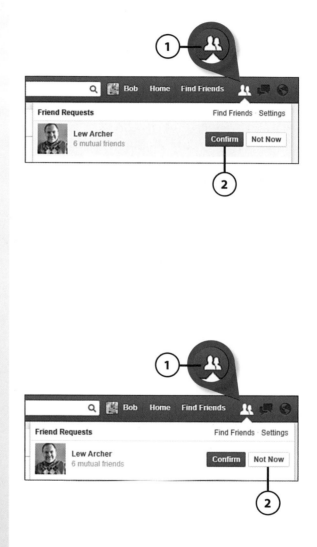

 (**1**) Click the Friend Request button on the Facebook toolbar. All pending friend requests are displayed in the drop-down menu.

(**2**) Click Confirm to accept a specific friend request and be added to that person's friends list.

Decline a Friend Request

You do not have to accept all friend requests. If you receive a request from someone you don't know (or someone you don't like), you can decline the request.

(**1**) Click the Friend Request button on the Facebook toolbar. All pending friend requests are displayed in the drop-down menu.

(**2**) Click Not Now to ignore the request.

No One Knows

When you decline a friend request, the sender is not notified by Facebook. That person doesn't know that you've declined the request, just that you haven't (yet) accepted it.

Unfriending Unwanted Friends

What do you do about those friends you really don't want to be friends with anymore? Sometimes people drift apart, or you don't like that person's political views or inane posts. Whatever the reason, you don't want to read any more of that person's posts, and you want to delete him from your friends list.

Unfriend a Friend

You can, at any time, remove any individual from your Facebook friends list. This is called *unfriending* the person, and it happens all the time.

No One's the Wiser

When you unfriend people on Facebook, they don't know that they've been unfriended. There are no official notices sent.

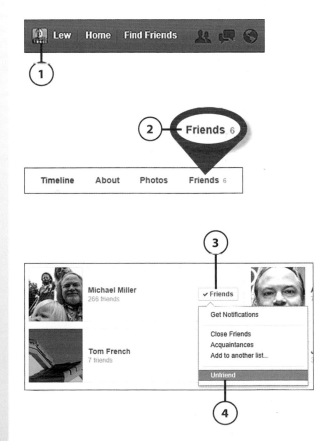

(**1**) Click your profile picture in the navigation sidebar or your name on the toolbar to display your Timeline page.

(**2**) Click Friends beneath your name to display your Friends page.

(**3**) Scroll to the person you want to unfriend, and mouse over the Friends button to display the pop-up menu.

(**4**) Select Unfriend.

Refriending

If you've unfriended someone but later want to add them back to your friends list, simply go through the add-a-friend process again.

Navigation
sidebar

News Feed

Status
update

In this chapter, you discover how to read and respond to your friends' status updates in your Facebook News Feed.

→ Viewing Updates in the News Feed
→ Viewing Status Updates
→ Responding to Status Updates

3

Discovering What Your Friends and Family Are Up To

After you've added someone to your Facebook friends list, you'll be kept up to date on what that person is doing and thinking. Everything that person posts to Facebook—text updates, photos, videos, you name it—automatically appears in your News Feed.

Viewing Updates in the News Feed

Facebook's News Feed is where you keep abreast of what all your friends are up to. When a person posts a status update to Facebook, it appears in your personal News Feed.

Display the News Feed

You can easily get to the News Feed from anywhere on the Facebook site, using the ever-present toolbar at the top of every Facebook page.

1. From the Facebook toolbar, click the Home button.

2. The News Feed displays in the center of the page. Note that in the navigation sidebar (left-side menu), the top item, News Feed, is selected. If you later choose to display other content (by clicking an item in the sidebar), you can return to the News Feed by clicking News Feed in the sidebar.

3. The News Feed lists what Facebook deems to be your most relevant or interesting posts at the top. Scroll down to view additional posts.

Display Most Recent Posts

By default, your News Feed displays what Facebook calls your Top Stories. These may not actually be the items you're most interested in, or even the most recent posts from your friends. You can, however, change the News Feed to display your friends' most recent posts.

(1) In the Facebook toolbar, click Home to display your home page and News Feed.

(2) To display the most recent posts, move to the navigation sidebar, click the down arrow next to the News Feed item, and then click Most Recent.

(3) To redisplay the most important posts, click the down arrow next to the News Feed item in the sidebar, and then click Top Stories.

>>>*Go Further*

TOP STORIES

By default, Facebook sorts the posts in your News Feed by importance—what it calls Top Stories. Facebook tries to determine what posts are most important to you, and puts them first in the feed.

The problem is, Facebook's idea of what's important might be different from what you think is important. Facebook's Top Stories sorting might actually bury posts from friends you really want to read—or not display them at all.

The solution to Facebook's arbitrary Top Stories sorting is to select the Most Recent feed. This sorts the updates in your feed in chronological order, putting the most recent posts at the top—period.

Viewing Status Updates

The News Feed consists of status updates made by your friends and by company and celebrity pages you've liked on Facebook. It also includes posts from Facebook groups you've joined, as well as the occasional advertisement.

View a Status Update

Each status update in your News Feed consists of several distinct components.

(1) The poster's profile picture appears in the top-left corner.

(2) The poster's name appears at the top of the post, beside the profile picture. To view more information about this person, mouse over his or her name; to view the poster's Timeline page, click the person's name.

(3) When the item was posted (how many minutes or hours or days ago) is displayed beneath the poster's name.

(4) The content of the status update appears under the top portion of the post. This can include text, images, or a video.

(5) Links to like, comment on, and share this post appear after the post content.

View Links to Web Pages

Many status updates include links to interesting web pages. You can click a link to view the web page posted by your friend.

(1) The title of the linked-to web page appears under the normal status update text. Click the title to display the linked-to web page in a new tab of your web browser.

(2) Many links include images from the linked-to page, as well as a short description of the page's content.

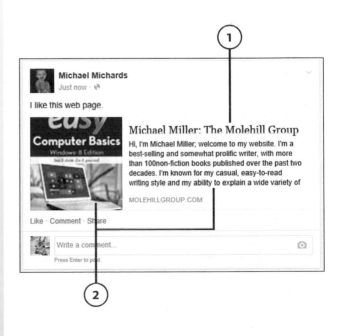

View Photos

It's common for Facebook users to post photos they've taken with their smartphones or digital cameras. These photos appear as part of the status update.

(1) The photo appears in the body of the status update.

(2) If more than one photo is posted, they may appear in a tiled collage or in side-scrolling display.

(3) To view a larger version of any picture, click the photo in the post.

(4) This displays the photo within its own *lightbox*—a special window superimposed over the News Feed. To close the photo lightbox, click the X in the upper-right corner.

View Videos

Many Facebook users post their own home movies so their friends can view them.

(1) A thumbnail image from the video appears in the body of the status update, with a "play" arrow superimposed on top of the image. Many videos start playing automatically when the post is viewed. For those that don't, click the image to play the video.

(2) If the video plays with the sound muted, mouse over the video to display the playback controls and then click the Volume (speaker) button and adjust the volume.

(3) To pause playback, mouse over the video and then click the Pause button.

(4) To view the video full screen, click the full screen button.

Responding to Status Updates

Facebook is a social network, which means you can interact socially with the status updates your friends make. You can tell your friend you "like" a given post, you can comment on a post, and you can even share a post with other friends.

Like an Update

When you "like" a friend's status update, you give it a virtual "thumbs up." It's like voting on a post; when you view a status update, you see the number of "likes" that post has received.

1. Click Like underneath the status update.

2. Other people who have liked this status update are listed under the post.

Dislike and Unlike

There is no corresponding "dislike" you can voice for posts you don't really like. However, when you like a post, the Like link changes to an Unlike link. If you later change your mind about a post, just click the Unlike link and your "like" goes away.

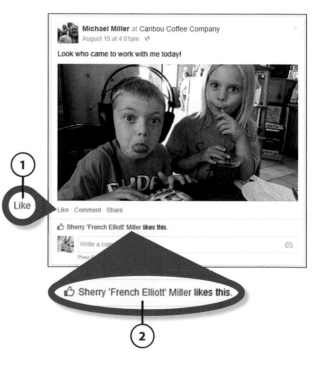

Comment on an Update

Sometimes you want to comment on a given post, to share your thoughts about the post with your friend. You do this by leaving a public comment, which can then be seen by others viewing the original post.

1 Although you can click the Comment link below the post, in most cases that isn't necessary. (You only need to click Comment if the Write a Comment box is not visible beneath the post.)

2 Type your comment into the Write a Comment box and press Enter.

3 Comments made by other users appear underneath the original post.

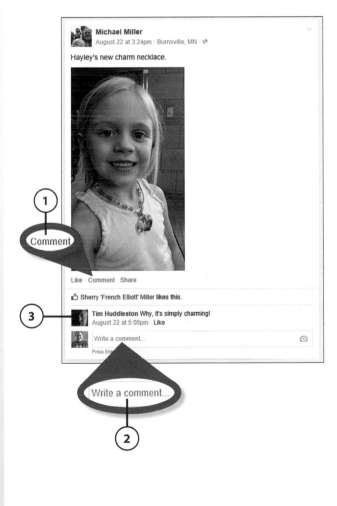

Share an Update

Occasionally, you'll find a status update that is interesting or intriguing enough you want to share it with all of your friends. You do this via Facebook's Share feature.

1. Click Share underneath the original post to display the Share This Status panel.

2. Click the Share button to display the list of options, and then select On Your Own Timeline to share it with your entire friends list. (This option is probably selected by default.)

3. Enter any comments you might have on this post into the Write Something area.

4. If you're sharing a text update, click the Share Status button. If you're sharing a photo, click the Share Photo button. If you're sharing a link to another web page, click the Share Link button.

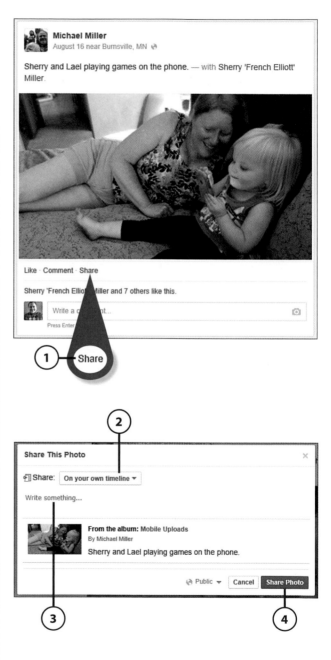

>>>Go Further

SHARE PRIVATELY

If you'd rather share a post privately with selected friends, click the Share button and select
In a Private Message. When the dialog box changes, enter the friends' names into the To
section, write a short message, and then click the Share Status button.

Facebook
meme

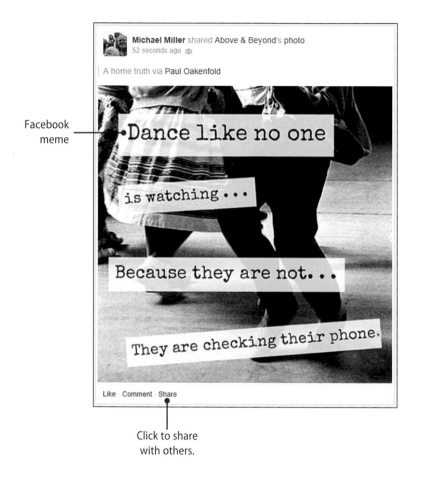

Michael Miller shared Above & Beyond's photo
52 seconds ago

A home truth via Paul Oakenfold

•Dance like no one

is watching . . .

Because they are not. . .

They are checking their phone.

Like · Comment · Share

Click to share
with others.

In this chapter, you discover what types of posts are the most popular among Facebook users.

→ Posts with Photos
→ Memes
→ Surveys
→ Countdown Lists
→ Links to Other Web Pages
→ Games

Exploring News Feed Posts

Everything goes in cycles—including Facebook posts. What was popular last year isn't so popular today.

The posts you're most likely to see in your News Feed reflect what other Facebook users like to see. Facebook uses a proprietary algorithm to determine what the "top stories" are in your Top Stories feed, but in general it's those types of posts that other users are most apt to like, share, or comment on.

What, then, is most likely to show up in your News Feed? It's all about things you can view at a glance.

Posts with Photos

Facebook started out as pretty much a text-only service; that is, you posted status updates that told your story in words, not pictures.

That's changed. Facebook, like most other media, has become more visual. This is due to the simple fact that most people prefer looking at pictures to reading text. We are a visual society, and Facebook reflects this.

In reality, this means that more people look at a post that contains a photo than one that's just text. You can still include that same text in a photo post, of course, but it's the picture that gets people's attention.

If you post that text *without* an accompanying photo, fewer friends look at it, and it's less likely that they'll even see it. That's because Facebook aims to show you posts that you and other users are more likely to interact with, and fewer people click Like or Comment or Share for text-only posts. Because fewer people interact with text-only posts, Facebook shows fewer of them in your News Feed.

So if you want your friends to see more of your posts, you need to post pictures in addition to your text. It certainly helps if the picture has something to do with what you're posting, and the more appealing the picture, the more eyeballs you'll attract. But the key thing is to get some sort of visual in as many posts as possible.

And that is why so many posts from your friends include pictures—all types of pictures.

(1) Many photos posted to Facebook are of the poster doing something interesting. Friends always like to see what you're up to.

2 Other photos are of things like the poster at an interesting location you've seen. Friends like to see where you've been.

3 Some people post pictures of a location—such as a night out on the town or a special vacation spot. Sometimes a good location photo is even more appealing than a picture with someone in it.

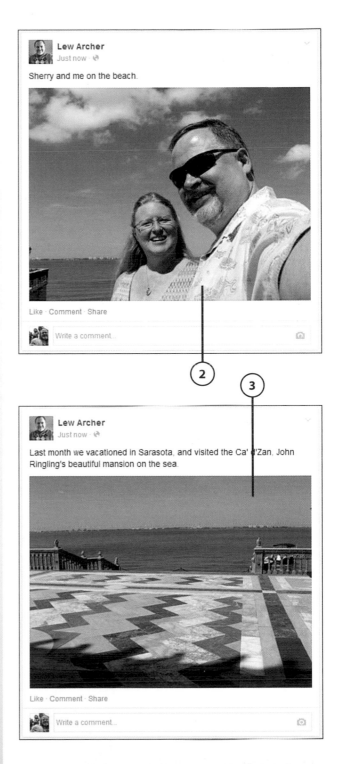

4 Lots of Facebookers post *selfies*—pictures you take of yourself, typically with your smartphone camera. Selfies can accompany any kind of post— even if you're just ranting about life in general, people will see a picture of you while you're ranting.

5 Of course, you'll see lots of people posting pictures of other people they're with—especially their kids and grandkids. Most people love to see cute pictures of young kids.

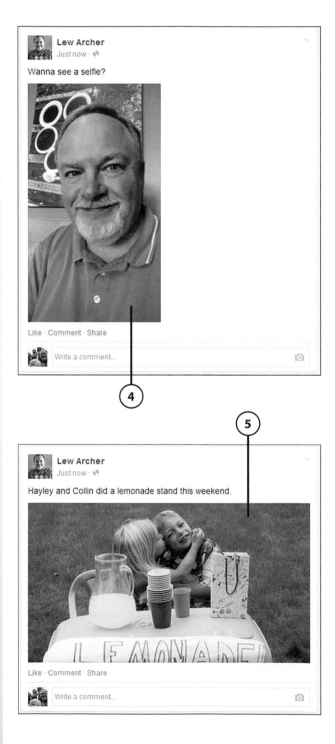

(6) Then there are those pictures that people post of their pets. Some (but certainly not all) people like to see cute pet pictures. (But not too many of them, please!)

Pictures for the Sake of Pictures

I know some Facebook users who simply attach random or mostly irrelevant photos to their posts, knowing that this alone will help them get placed in more of their friends' News Feeds. But it's better if the images you use have something to do with what you're posting about.

Lew Archer
Just now ·

Our dog Kaylee, on the run.

Like · Comment · Share

Write a comment...

(6)

Memes

A lot of what you see on Facebook are posts that others have seen in their News Feeds, and then shared with their friends. When a post gets shared and shared and shared again, it becomes *viral*—that is, it spreads quickly from person-to-person, kind of like a virus does in the real world. Viral posts on Facebook, however, aren't dangerous. Mostly, they're fun.

The most popular viral posts get repeated so often that they become *memes*. A meme is a concept or catchphrase or image that spreads in a viral fashion over the Internet. Some memes are repeated exactly, but most are adaptable in different ways.

While memes are essentially passing fads, they do get a lot of likes and shares, which boosts their popularity on Facebook. Chances are a meme you see in your News Feed today (and tomorrow and the next day) will wear out its welcome in a few weeks.

1 Most Facebook memes are pictures of something familiar or someone famous, with humorous text superimposed on the image. You may see multiple instances of that same meme, with different humorous text on the same picture.

2 Many memes use pictures of cute or ugly animals to humorous effect.

3. Some memes, like the "what people think I do" meme, use multiple pictures to get the point across.

4. Some memes are just funny sayings accompanied by a generic or ironic illustration, kind of like a funny greeting card.

Surveys

A specific type of meme that has become increasingly popular of late is the survey. This typically consists of a picture that boasts the results of someone taking the survey; you're prompted to click the picture or link to take the survey yourself.

Most of these surveys are fun and not very scientific. There's little harm in taking one of these surveys, other than the time you waste doing so. The results are most often generic and seldom reflect any deep insights into your life or character.

(1) Most surveys in your News Feed reflect lifestyle or general interest topics, such as "What color are you?" or "Which celebrity should play you in a movie?" or "What Star Trek character are you?" Click the link to take the survey.

(2) The survey itself asks you a series of seemingly unrelated questions, each on its own web page. Make a selection and move to the next page until the survey is completed.

(3) At the end of the survey you discover just which color you are, or whatever the survey is supposed to determine. You're then prompted to share this earth-shattering information on Facebook. If you click the Facebook button, the survey result is posted to your News Feed for all your friends to see.

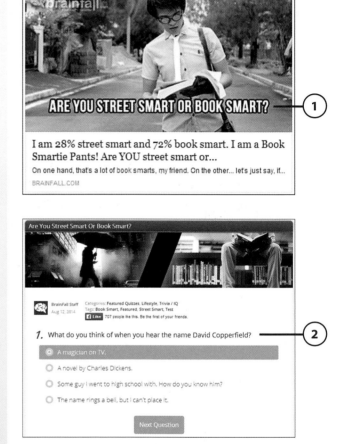

Countdown Lists

Another popular type of post is actually common all across the Web, not just on Facebook. This is the quasi-informational post that purports to tell you X number of things about a given topic, in the form of a countdown list. These posts come with sensational headlines designed to grab you and pull you in, such as "18 Reasons We'll Always Be Crazy for Patrick Swayze" or "10 Bad Movie Ideas" or "12 Best Celebrity Beach Bodies."

What these posts do is take you to another website, where each of the X number of things has its own page. You have to click from page to page to view all the items on the countdown list, and each page is chock full of ads. It's all a big scam to get you to click one of the ads (either on purpose or accidentally) so the host site can generate money from that advertising. There's no actual harm done—again, it's just a waste of your time.

Clickbait

Countdown lists and similar posts are often called *clickbait*, because they "bait" you into clicking to learn more. Facebook is trying to crack down on this type of clickbait; if the company is successful, you'll see fewer of these annoying posts in your News Feed.

---

(1) A typical countdown list post starts with an attention-grabbing headline. Click the headline to go to the hosting website, typically in a new browser tab.

12 Times Dogs Proved They're Actually Heroes
Name one thing better than a dog. See? You can't.
BUZZFEED.COM | BY ALEX ALVAREZ

(2) Each item in the countdown list typically has its own web page, or is part of a long scrolling page. All that space is an opportunity to serve you a plethora of annoying web ads.

BuzzFeed

A surprising number of these countdown clickbait posts link to stories on the BuzzFeed website (www.buzzfeed.com). BuzzFeed is notorious for posting salacious quasi-news stories and multi-page countdown lists—it's a kind of yellow journalism for the Internet age.

Links to Other Web Pages

Many of your Facebook friends post links to other interesting information on the Web. A post with a web page link is typically accompanied by a thumbnail image from that page, so the post is visual and gets your attention.

(1) A post with a link to a web page typically includes an image from that page and the title of that page. Posts can link to traditional web pages or to articles on the Web.

2 Click the image or title of the link and you now see the linked-to web page, typically in a new tab in your web browser. Close that tab to return to Facebook.

Games

One of the other types of posts you're likely to see a lot comes from the Face-book games that your friends play. These games post your friends' most recent scores and any free items they've won—or even beg you to play the game yourself.

1 Posts from Facebook's social games typically include an image from the game and information about your friend's recent play.

2 Click the image or title to sign up to play.

3 If these types of posts annoy you, you can choose to hide them in your News Feed. Mouse over the post, click the down arrow at the top-right corner, then click Hide All From this game.

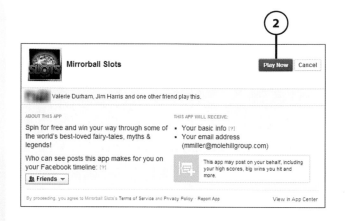

>>>*Go Further*

THE IMPORTANCE OF SHARING

An increasing number of posts on Facebook are not original posts—they're items that other people have seen on Facebook (and elsewhere) that they've decided to share in their News Feed. This type of sharing is what makes Facebook a social network, and also what can make a given post go viral. When someone shares a post with you and you share it with your friends and they share with their friends—well, you see how quickly something can be spread around.

To share a post you like, click Share beneath the post. You can add your own comments to the post or share it as-is. You can also choose to share the post with your entire friends list (On Your Own Timeline) or with selected friends or groups. There's no need to feel shy about sharing; everyone on Facebook does it!

Just try not to share too many of those posts that other people find annoying. The occasional meme or survey is fine and fun in its own way, but if you flood your friends' News Feeds with too many of these frivolous items, you might find that they're not your friends any more. Be judicious about what you share—and try not to waste your friends' time.

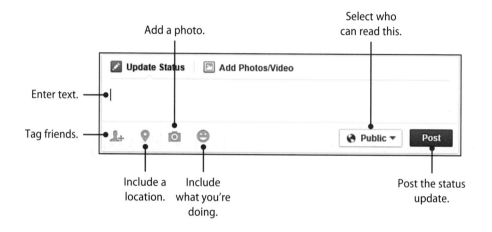

Add a photo.

Select who
can read this.

Enter text.

Tag friends.

Include a
location.

Include
what you're
doing.

Post the status
update.

In this chapter, you learn how to post Facebook status updates for others to read.

→ Updating Your Status
→ Sharing Content from Other Websites

Updating Friends and Family on Your Activities

To let your family and friends know what you've been up to, you need to post what Facebook calls a *status update*. Every status update you make is broadcast to everyone on your friends list, displayed in the News Feed on their home pages. It's how they know what you've been doing and thinking about.

Updating Your Status

A status update is, at its most basic, a brief text message. It can be as short as a word or two, or it can be several paragraphs long; that's up to you. (Facebook lets you post updates with more than 60,000 characters, which should be more than long enough for most of us.)

Although a basic status update is all text, you can also attach other items to your status updates, including digital photographs, videos, and links to other web pages. You can also "tag" other Facebook users and groups in your updates, so that their names appear as clickable links (to their Timeline pages).

Tags

A *tag* is a way to mention other Facebook users in your status updates and photos. When a person is tagged in a post, the post appears in that person's Facebook feed, so he knows you're talking about him. In addition, readers can click a tagged name to display that person's Timeline page.

Post a Basic Status Update

Facebook makes it easy to post a status update. You have to be signed in to your Facebook account; then it's a simple matter of opening your home page and creating the post.

1. Click the Home button on the Facebook toolbar to return to your home page.

2. Go to the Publisher box (labeled What's On Your Mind?) at the top of the page. Note that the Update Status tab is selected by default.

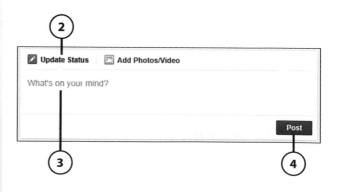

3. Type your message into the What's On Your Mind? box. The Publisher box expands to display a series of option buttons at the bottom.

4. Click the Post button when you're done.

Other Ways to Update

You can also post status updates from the Publisher box located on your Facebook Timeline page, from the Facebook app on your smartphone or tablet, or via text message from your cell phone.

>>>*Go Further*

HASHTAGS

Facebook offers the option of including *hashtags* in your status updates. A hashtag is like a keyword, a word or phrase that describes the content of your post—and that readers can click to see similar posts with the same hashtag. A hashtag starts with the hash (#) character, followed by the keyword or phrase (with no spaces between the words).

Hashtags were made popular by Twitter, another popular social network. They've never really caught on with Facebook users, however, so you shouldn't bother with including hashtags in your own posts. If you see a hashtag in a friend's status update, you can click it to display a list of other posts that include the same hashtag.

Post a Link to a Web Page

You can include links to other web pages in your status updates. Facebook adds a link to the specified page, and it also lets you include a thumbnail image from that page with the status update.

(1) Start a new post as normal, and enter any accompanying text.

(2) Enter the URL (web address) for the page you want to link to as part of your update.

(3) Facebook should recognize the link and display a Link panel, complete with thumbnail image from the page. (If the web page doesn't include any pictures, you won't see a thumbnail image.) Click the left and right arrows to select one of multiple thumbnail images to accompany the link.

(4) If you don't want to display an image from the page, click the X in the top-right corner of the thumbnail image.

(5) Click the Post button when done.

Delete the URL

If you don't want to display the web page's URL in the body of your status update, you can delete the address after the Link panel appears. The link and accompanying image still display under your status update even after you delete the web page URL from your text.

Status   Add Photos/Video

He   good source of learning materials: www.pearson.com

Pearson - Always Learning

Pearson is the world's leading learning company. We have 36,000 people in more than 70 countries, helping people of all ages to make progress in their

WWW.PEARSON.COM

Public ▾   Post

Post a Photograph or Video

Facebook enables you to embed digital photographs and videos in your posts. It's the Facebook equivalent of attaching a file to an email message.

1. Go to the Publisher box and click Add Photos/Video. This presents two new options for your new status update.

2. Click Upload Photos/Video to display the Choose File to Upload or Open dialog box. (Which dialog box displays depends on which web browser you're using.)

3. Navigate to and select the photo or video file(s) you want to upload. You can upload a single video file or multiple photo files; to select more than one file, hold down the Ctrl key while you click each filename.

4. Click the Open button.

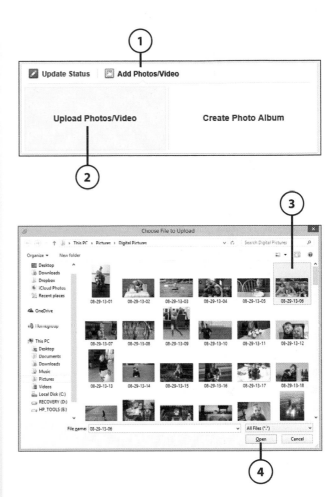

5 You're returned to the Publisher box with your photo(s) added. Click the + icon to add another picture, if you want.

6 If you like, enter a short text message describing the photo(s) or video.

7 Click the Post button.

Create a Photo Album

By default, photos you upload as status updates are added to your Timeline Photos album on Facebook. If you'd rather create a new photo album for an uploaded photo, select Create Photo Album instead of Upload Photos/Video and follow the onscreen instructions from there.

Photo added to status update

Add Your Location to a Post

Facebook enables you to identify your current location in any post you make. This lets your friends know where you are at any given time.

1 Enter the text of your status update into the Publisher box as normal, or select any photos you want to post.

2 Click the Add a Location to Post button beneath the Publisher box.

3. If Facebook can tell your location automatically, it displays a list of options. Otherwise, start entering your location manually; as you type, Facebook displays a list of suggested locations, along with a map of the current selection.

4. Click the correct location from the resulting list.

5. Click the Post button.

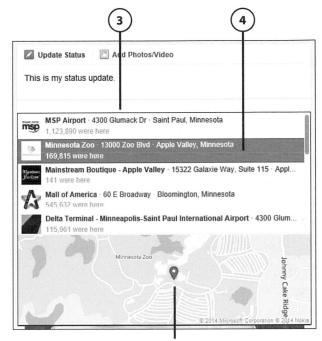

Map of selected location

Location added to post

It's Not All Good

Don't Publicize Your Location

You might not want to identify your location on every post you make. If you post while you're away from home, you're letting potential burglars know that your house is empty. You're also telling potential stalkers where they can find you. For these reasons, use caution when posting your location in your status updates.

Tag a Friend in a Post

Sometimes you might want to mention one of your friends in a status update, or include a friend who was with you when the post was made. You can do this by "tagging" friends in your status updates; the resulting post includes a link to the tagged person or persons.

(1) Enter the text of your status update into the Publisher box as normal, or any photos you want to post.

(2) Click the Tag People in Your Post button beneath the Publisher box.

(3) Enter the name of the person you want to tag. As you type, Facebook displays a drop-down list with matching names from your Facebook friends list.

(4) Select the friend from the list.

(5) Click the Post button.

Tagged Friends

Clicking a tagged person's name in a status update displays the Facebook Timeline page for that person.

Tell Friends What You're Doing

Given the huge number of posts in which people write about what they're doing at the moment, Facebook has added a Say What You Are Doing option to its status updates. This provides a very quick way to tell your friends what you're doing.

(1) Enter the text of your status update into the Publisher box as normal. (Or, if you're just posting what you're doing, leave the Publisher box empty.)

(2) Click the Say What You Are Doing button beneath the Publisher box.

(3) Facebook displays a list of actions—including Feeling, Watching, Reading, Listening To, Drinking, Eating, Playing, Traveling To, Looking For, and Exercising. If what you're doing is not listed, type it into the What Are You Doing? box above the drop-down menu, and then press Enter.

(4) Otherwise, click the action that best describes what you're doing to display a list of options specific to that action.

(1)

✐ Update Status	🖾 Add Photos/Video

This is my status update.

What are you doing?

👤 📍 📷 😊   🌐 Public ▾   **Post**

(2)——😊

(3)

✐ Update Status	🖾 Add Photos/Video

This is my status update.

|

😊	Feeling	▸
👓	Watching	▸
📖	Reading	▸
🎧	Listening To	▸
🥤	**Drinking**	▸
🍴	Eating	▸
🎮	Playing	▸
✈	Traveling To	▸
◯	Looking For	▸

(4)

5 Select the appropriate option for what you're doing.

6 Finish the rest of your status update as usual, and then click the Post button.

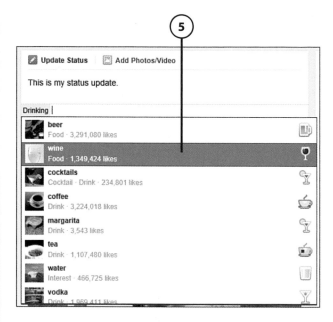

What you're doing

Determine Who Can— or Can't—See a Status Update

By default, the items you post to Facebook can be seen by everyone on your friends list. If you'd rather send a given post to a more select group of people, or to everyone on the site, you can change the privacy settings for any individual post. This enables only selected people to see that post; other people on your friends list won't see it at all.

(**1**) Enter the text of your status update, or any photos you want to upload, into the Publisher box as normal.

(**2**) Click the Privacy button (the second button from the right beneath the post) to display a list of privacy options.

(**3**) Click Public to let everyone on Facebook see the post.

(**4**) Click Friends to make a post visible only to people on your friends list.

(**5**) Click More Options to view more privacy options.

6 Click Only Me to make the post only visible to yourself—no one else will be able to see it.

7 In the bottom section of the menu list, click the name of a specific friends list to make a post visible only to the friends on that list.

8 To select specific individuals who can or can't view this post, click Custom; this displays the Custom Privacy panel.

9 Go to the Share This With section and make a selection from the These People or Lists list to make this post visible to specific friends, friends lists, or networks.

10 To *hide* this post from specific friends or friends lists, go to the Don't Share This With section and enter names into the These People or Lists box.

11 Click the Save Changes button.

12 Back in your post, click the Post button to send this status update to those people you've selected.

Configure Privacy for All Your Posts

Although you can configure the privacy option for each post you make individually, you can also set universal privacy settings that affect all your status updates. Learn more in Chapter 18, "Managing Your Privacy on Facebook."

>>>*Go Further*

POSTING ETIQUETTE

Writing a Facebook status update is a bit like sending a text message on your cell phone. As such, status updates do not have to—and often don't—conform to proper grammar, spelling, and sentence structure. It's common to abbreviate longer words, use familiar acronyms, substitute single letters and numbers for whole words, and refrain from all punctuation.

Then there's the issue of how often you should update your Facebook status. Unfortunately, there are no hard and fast rules as to posting frequency. Some people post once a week, others post daily, others post several times a day. In general, you should post when you have something interesting to share—and not because you feel obligated to make a post.

Sharing Content from Other Websites

Facebook is all about sharing things with your friends. Naturally, you can share your thoughts and activities via status updates; you can also upload and share your personal photos and videos.

But Facebook is also connected to many other sites on the Web. This enables you to share content you find elsewhere with your Facebook friends. It's all about posting content from other websites to your Facebook Timeline—and your friends' News Feeds.

Post Content from Another Site

Many websites would like you to share their content with your friends on Facebook. When you're browsing another site and find something interesting to share, look for a Facebook button. This button is sometimes included in a special "sharing" section of the page; it's often labeled Facebook, Facebook Share, Facebook Like, or Facebook Recommend.

News Sharing

Facebook sharing buttons are especially common on news-type sites, which makes it easy to share the articles you find there.

(1) Click the Facebook button on the other website. (If you're currently signed into your Facebook account, you probably won't need to log in again. However, if you're prompted to sign into your Facebook account at this point, enter your email address and password, and then click the Log In button.)

(2) What you see next depends on the site. In some instances, the link to the page is posted automatically without any comments from you. In other instances, you have the option of including a personal comment with the link; enter your comment, and then click the Share, Share Link, Post, or Add a Comment button, depending on what you see.

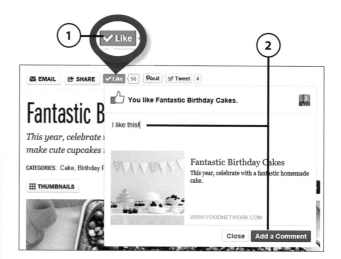

Short text message

Photo

Michael Miller
7 hrs · Burnsville, MN · 🌐

Your dose of cuteness for the day. Granddaughter Hayley plays dress up. Or something.

Like · Comment · Share

👍 Sherry 'French Elliott' Miller and Heidi Haskins like this.

Write a comment... 📷

Press Enter to post.

In this chapter, you discover the types of things you should share on Facebook—and those you shouldn't.

→ What's Good to Post on Facebook
→ What *Not* to Post on Facebook
→ Learning Facebook Etiquette

6

What You Should—and Shouldn't—Share on Facebook

Facebook is not your own private diary or soapbox. It's a public website, where what you post is visible to all your friends and family—and, potentially, millions of other users.

As such, it's important to make your posts interesting to the people who'll be reading them. It's also important not to post certain types of information; with everyone you know—or may know in the future—reading everything you post, it's easy to get yourself in trouble with a few taps of the computer keyboard.

What's Good to Post on Facebook

If you've been on Facebook for any time at all, you've seen your share of boring, self-indulgent, and useless status updates from friends. Not everyone has the knack for posting updates that you really want to read.

It's important to post interesting status updates. But what, exactly, qualifies as something worthwhile to post about?

Post Interesting Information

The best advice I can give for what to post on Facebook is anything that your friends and family are likely to find interesting. Not things you might find interesting, but what others might find interesting about you.

Interesting Topics

To make sure your updates get read, focus on interesting and unique topics. The fact that you went to a concert or read a good book is interesting; that you woke up with a headache or just had a cup of tea is not.

(1) Post things you want to share with your Facebook friends. These are moments and events that are not only important to you, but also are things you think your friends might care about, too.

(2) Post things that your friends and family want to know about. Friends typically want to know if you've done or seen something interesting, taken a vacation, met a mutual friend, and such. If you think someone's interested in it, post it.

(1)

Lew Archer
Just now ·

Had a wonderful time visiting with all our old friends in San Diego last week. Great weather and great conversations all week long!

Like · Comment · Share

Write a comment...

Lew Archer
Just now ·

All you old westsiders, I ran into Gene Swift at the coffeehouse last night. He's still playing golf at the Westside Club, says hi to everybody.

Like · Comment · Share

(2)

3 Post about major life events—things in your life that your friends and family *need* to know about. These are important moments and events, such as anniversaries, birthdays, and celebrations.

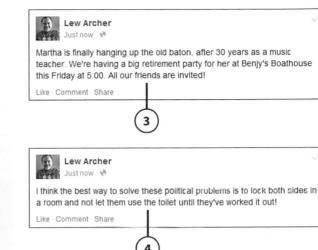

4 Post interesting thoughts. Share your wisdom with your friends and family via Facebook status updates—in a noncontroversial, inoffensive way, if you can.

Post Important Information

Many people use Facebook as a kind of bulletin board for their families and friends. One post can inform a large number of people about something important; it's a lot more efficient than sending out dozens of emails or making tons of phone calls. Again—for privacy reasons, be cautious about what you share and with whom.

1 Post if something has happened to you. If you've been ill or hospitalized, lost your job, moved to a new house, or whatever, use Facebook to let everyone know about it.

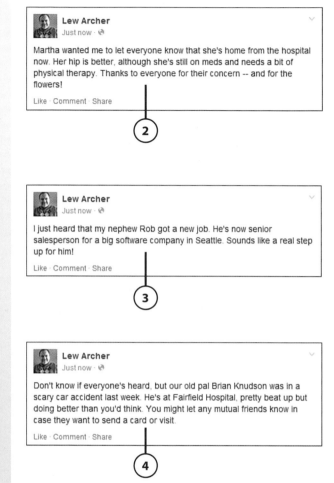

② Post if something has happened to your spouse or partner. Many of your friends are likely mutual friends, so if anything major has happened, include that information in your status update—especially if your spouse or partner can't post, for whatever reason.

③ Post if something has happened to another family member. You might know something about a cousin or nephew that others in your family might not know about. Share your information with other family members via a Facebook post.

④ Post if something has happened to a mutual friend. It's tough to keep track of all your old friends. Start the chain going by posting what you know, and let your other friends pass it on to their friends, too.

What *Not* to Post on Facebook

There are some things you probably shouldn't post on Facebook. Many of the posts you see from friends are mundane and uninteresting; some are inflammatory and offensive. And then there are those posts that just contain too much information about personal matters you'd rather not know.

It's important, then, to think before you post. Remember that Facebook is not a private diary; it's a public website with more than 1 billion users. Some things simply shouldn't be shared with all those people.

Avoid Uninteresting or Unwise Posts

Remember, by default, Facebook status updates are public for all to read. Post only that information that you'd want your friends (or spouse or grandkids) to read.

- Don't complain. The last thing your Facebook friends want to find in their News Feeds is your private griping. It's okay to grouse and be grumpy from time to time (you're entitled), but don't use Facebook as your personal forum for petty grievances. If you have a personal problem, deal with it; whining gets old really fast. (We especially don't want to hear if you're having a fight with your partner or problems with your kids. This sort of thing is best kept private.)

- Keep your opinions to yourself. In particular, avoid getting overly political or controversial in your posts. It's true that some people like to use Facebook as a platform for their opinions, but that's a sure fire way to get "unfriended" by people who disagree with you. Although it might be okay to share your opinions with close real world friends, spouting off in a public forum is not only bad form; it's a way to incite a flame war—an unnecessary online war of words.

- Don't post confessions. Facebook is not the place to come clean about past indiscretions; it's a public forum, not a private confessional. If you need to confess something to someone, do it in a more private way.

- Don't get too personal. Facebook is definitely not the best place to share intimate details about your life. Most people feel a little awkward when someone discloses just a little too much about his or her personal life. A good rule of thumb is that if you don't want your kids or grandkids to know about it, don't share it on Facebook.

- Don't post anything that anyone—including lawyers, employers, or the police—could use against you. When you post a status update, it's there for everyone to see, friend or foe. It gets back to that confessional thing; if you think something could come back to bite you, don't post it.

- Don't post embarrassing photos of yourself or others, and don't tag anyone else who might be in those photos—especially your children or grandchildren. You don't want to humiliate yourself or your family online.

- Don't post just to get attention. Here's something new to Facebook: *vague-booking*. This is the practice of posting a message that's intentionally vague but hints at some personal problem or crisis (such as "Life is so unfair. You know who I'm talking about."). People vaguebook to get their friends to respond with worried inquiries about what's wrong; it's highly manipulative and sure to create enmity over time. If you really have some sort of problem, it's better to call a friend instead of posting about it publicly to everyone on Facebook.

- Don't post if you don't have anything interesting to say. Posting too many meaningless updates will cause friends to start ignoring everything you post.

Avoid Posting Personal Information

There's a whole other class of information you shouldn't post on Facebook—personal information that could be used by identity thieves to hijack your bank accounts or site memberships online. If you don't want to become a victim of identity theft, avoid posting too many personal details to your Facebook account.

- *Don't* post your personal contact information—phone number, street address, email address, and so forth. You don't want complete strangers to contact or harass you.

- *Don't* post location information when you're away from home. This can tip off burglars that your house is empty, or notify stalkers where you can be found. Wait until after you get home to share where you had dinner or vacationed.

- *Don't* post the layout of your house. You don't want to give potential burglars a roadmap to all your goodies.

- *Don't* post your Social Security number (SSN). Ever. If your SSN gets in the wrong hands, identity theft will result.

- *Don't* post other pieces of information that could be used to gain access to your online accounts—your birthdate, birthplace, mother's maiden name, and so forth. This information is typically used for "challenge questions" if you forget your password on a website; if you post this information where potential thieves can see it, they might be able to reset your password and gain access to your online accounts.

Learning Facebook Etiquette

Your status updates on Facebook should be not only interesting but also easy to read. Not that each post has to be letter perfect, but there are some guidelines you should follow.

Carefully Compose Your Status Updates

Facebook status updates are not long, thought-out missives. A status update is more immediate than an email, and less well-constructed than a handwritten letter.

That said, more people will read your posts if you follow some simple guidelines. Your status updates don't have to be perfect, but they do need to be in the ballpark.

- Be personal and personable. Your writing on Facebook should be light and informal, not stiff and professional. Write as you'd talk, in your own personal voice. Make it sound like you—and be as friendly as you know how to be.

- Keep your posts short. Facebook users, even your dear old friends, don't have the attention span, the patience, or the inclination to read long tomes. They want quick bits of information, something they can scan without necessarily reading. Keep each status update to a paragraph, no more than a few sentences—and the shorter the better.

- Include links and photos in your posts. A Facebook status update doesn't have to be just text. You can—and should—include photos and links to other websites in your posts. In fact, most posts today have some sort of visual element. Nothing wrong with text-only posts; it's just that users are drawn to—and tend to expect—more visually interesting posts. This means that people are more likely to ignore text-only posts in favor of posts with some sort of image. If you can illustrate your point with a photo, or a link to a picture on another web page, then do so.

Know the Shorthand

As anyone of a younger generation will no doubt attest, writing a Facebook status update is a bit like sending a text message on your cell phone. You do it quickly, without a lot of preparation or editing. It's an in-the-moment communication, and as such you can't be expected to take the time to create a grammatically perfect message.

For this reason, Facebook status updates do not have to—and seldom do—conform to proper grammar, spelling, and sentence structure. It's common to abbreviate longer words, use familiar acronyms, substitute single letters and numbers for whole words, and refrain from all punctuation.

For example, instead of spelling out the word "Friday," you can just write "Fri." Instead of saying "See you later," just say "later." Instead of spelling out "New York City," use the abbreviation "NYC."

Misspellings

It's also acceptable, at least to some users, to have the occasional misspelling. It's not something I personally like to do or see, but I'm a professional writer and pickier about these things than many people; most people will let it slide if you get the spelling or grammar wrong once in a while.

Younger users, especially, like to use a sort of online shorthand (or "Facebook grammar") to pack as much as possible into a short status update. These are the same acronyms and abbreviations that have been used for decades in text messaging, instant messaging, and Internet chat rooms. You might not be familiar with this shorthand, much of which is detailed in Table 6.1. It may be a tad unseemly for older folks to use this hip lingo, but it certainly helps to know what everything means when you're reading posts from your kids or grandkids.

Table 6.1   Common Facebook Acronyms

Acronym	Description
AFAIK	As far as I know
ASAP	As soon as possible
ASL	Age/sex/location
B/W	Between
B4	Before
BC	Because
BFN	Bye for now
BR	Best regards
BRB	Be right back
BTW	By the way
CU	See you
Cuz	Because
FB	Facebook
FTF	Face to face
FWIW	For what it's worth
FYI	For your information
GM	Good morning
GN	Good night
HTH	Hope that helps
IDK	I don't know
IM	Instant message
IMHO	In my humble opinion
IRL	In real life
JK	Just kidding
K	Okay
L8	Late
L8r	Later
LMAO	Laughing my ass off

Acronym	Description
LMK	Let me know
LOL	Laughing out loud
NSFW	Not safe for work
OH	Overheard
OMG	Oh my God
Pls *or* Plz	Please
Ppl *or* peeps	People
R	Are
Rly	Really
ROFL	Rolling on the floor laughing
SD	Sweet dreams
Tht	That
Thx *or* Tnx	Thanks
TY	Thank you
TTYL	Talk to you later
U	You
Ur	Your
WTF	What the f**k
WTH	What the hell
YMMV	Your mileage may vary
YW	You're welcome
Zzz	Sleeping

>>>Go Further

HOW OFTEN SHOULD YOU POST?

How often should you update your Facebook status? That's an interesting question, without a defined answer.

Some of my Facebook friends post frequently—several times a day. Some only post occasionally, once a month or so. Most, however, post once a day or once every few days. So if there's an average, that's it.

Some of the more frequent posters are justified, in that they post a lot of interesting information. Other frequent posters I find more annoying, in that their posts are more personal and less practical; every little tic and burp is immortalized in its own update. That's probably posting too much.

On the other hand, my friends who only post once a month or so probably aren't trying hard enough. I'd like to hear from them more often; certainly they're doing something interesting that's worth posting about. After a while, I tend to forget that they're still around.

So you need to post often enough that your friends don't forget about you, but not so often that they wish you'd just shut up. I suppose your update frequency has something to do with what it is you're doing, and how interesting that is. But it's okay to post just to let people know you're still there—as long as you don't do so hourly.

Photo lightbox

Information pane

In this chapter, you find out how to view photos uploaded by your friends to Facebook and how to upload your own photos for your friends to see.

→ Viewing Friends' Photos
→ Sharing Your Photos with Friends
→ Editing Your Photos and Albums

Viewing and Sharing Family Photos

Sharing pictures is a great way to catch up your friends and family on what you've been up to. Everybody loves looking at pictures—whether they're vacation photos or photos of your cute kids or grandkids.

Before everybody got on the Internet, if you wanted to share photos you had to make prints and mail them out to everyone, or invite everybody over to your house for an old-fashioned slide show. Today, however, you can share your photos online—via Facebook.

It should come as no surprise that Facebook is the largest photo-sharing site on the Internet. It's easy to upload photos to a Facebook photo album and then share them with all your Facebook friends. It's equally easy to view your friends' photos on Facebook—and download and print those you'd like to keep for posterity.

Viewing Friends' Photos

Some people on Facebook post photos as part of their regular status updates. These photos appear in your News Feed, as part of the stream of your friends' status updates.

Other Facebook users post photos to special photo albums they've created in the Facebook accounts. This is a more serious and organized way to share a large number of photos online. You can view these photo albums from the user's Timeline page.

View Photos in Your News Feed

When a friend posts a photo as part of a status update, that photo appears in your News Feed. You can view photos at that small size within the News Feed, or enlarge them to view them full screen.

① Within your News Feed, all photos appear within the bodies of the accompanying status updates. To view a larger version of any picture, click the photo in the post. This displays the photo within its own *lightbox*—a special window superimposed over the News Feed.

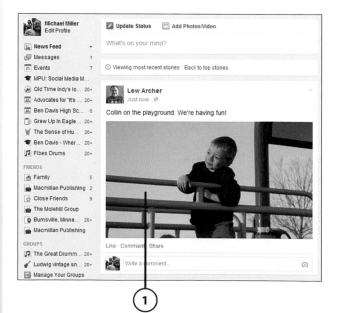

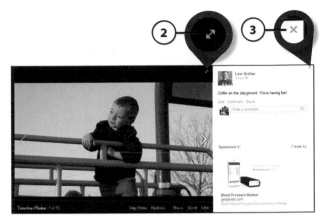

2 To view the photo even larger, click the Enter Fullscreen icon at the top-right corner of the photo. (To exit fullscreen mode, press Esc on your computer keyboard or the X at the top-right corner of the screen.)

3 To close the photo viewer, click the X in the upper-right corner, or press Esc on your keyboard.

View a Friend's Photo Albums

More serious photographers—and people with a lot of photos to share—organize their Facebook photos into separate photo albums. These are virtual versions of those traditional photo albums you've kept in the past. You can then navigate through a friend's photo albums to find and view the photos you like.

1 Click your friend's name or profile picture anywhere on Facebook to open his Timeline page.

Michael Miller
Yesterday at 3:07pm ·

Your information nugget du jour: Want to know what the younguns are doing when they leave Facebook? Then check out my article for Que Publishing about the latest social media for the younger generation, titled After Facebook: Examining Today's Hottest Social Media.

2 Click Photos under the person's name to display your friend's Photos page.

3 Click Photos of *Friend* to view all photos of your friend.

4 Click *Friend's* Photos to view all photos posted by your friend.

5 Click Albums to view photos as posted in their photo albums.

6 Click to open the selected album.

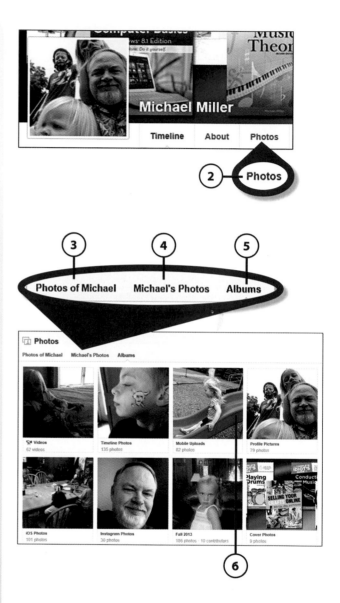

7 Click the thumbnail of the picture you want to view. Facebook displays the selected picture in a lightbox superimposed on top of the previous page.

8 Mouse over the current picture to display the navigational arrows; click the right arrow to go to the next picture or click the left arrow to go to the previous picture.

9 To close the photo viewer, click the X at the top right of the lightbox.

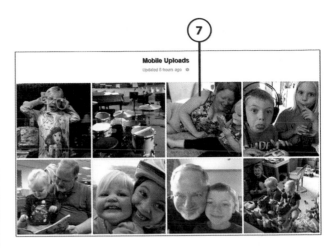

Comment On and Like a Photo

If you'd like to say something about a given photo, enter your comments on the photo page. When others view this photo, they also see your comment.

(1) Click to display the photo in the photo viewer.

(2) Enter your comments into the Write a Comment box, and then press Enter when done.

(3) Click Like to "like" a photo without entering any comments about it.

Share a Photo

If you really like a given photo you see in your News Feed, you can share that photo with your Facebook friends—with your own description.

1 Display the photo in the photo viewer and click the Share link; this displays the Share This Photo panel.

2 Click the Share button and select On Your Own Timeline. (This should be selected by default.)

3 Enter a description of the photo into the Say Something About This box.

4 Click the Privacy button and select who can view this photo: Public, Friends, Only Me, or Custom.

5 Click the Share Photo button to post this picture to your timeline.

> With two of my favorite girls on a fine summer morning.
> — at Keller Lake.
>
> Like · Comment · Share

1 — Share

2

Share This Photo   ×

Share: On your own timeline ▾

From the album: Mobile Uploads
By Michael Miller

With two of my favorite girls on a fine summer morning.

Public ▾   Cancel   Share Photo

3   **4**   **5**

>>>Go Further

SHARING PRIVATELY

You can also share a photo privately with another user or group of users. When the Share This Photo dialog box appears, click the Share button (which is set to On Your Own Timeline by default) and select to share On a Friend's Timeline, In a Group, On a Page You Manage, or In a Private Message. Select this last option to share the photo with a specific individual.

Tag Yourself in a Friend's Photo

If you find yourself in a photo that a friend has taken and uploaded to Facebook, you can "tag" yourself in that photo. When you're tagged in a photo, that photo appears in your Facebook timeline and on your Facebook photo albums page, in the Photos and Videos of You section.

(1) Display the photo in the photo viewer, mouse over the photo to display the menu at the bottom of the photo, and then click Tag Photo.

(2) Click your face in the photo. A box appears around your face.

(3) You now see a text box under the photo, with a list of matching names. Click your name in the list, or enter your name into the text box.

4 Your name is now tagged to your face in this photo. Click Done Tagging to finish.

Click on the photo to start tagging. **Done Tagging**

4

Remove Your Name from a Photo—or Remove the Photo

You might not want to be tagged in a given picture. Perhaps the photo shows you doing something you shouldn't be doing. Maybe the photo is just a bad picture you don't particularly like. Or maybe you just don't like your name or face being out there on the Internet without your permission. In any instance, Facebook enables you to remove your name from any photo tagged by a friend; you can even request that a given photo be completely removed from the Facebook site.

(**1**) Display the photo and mouse over the photo to display the menu at the bottom of the photo.

(**2**) To remove your tag from this photo, click Options, and then click Remove Tag. This displays the Remove Tag panel.

(**3**) To remove your tag but leave the photo on Facebook, click Okay.

(**4**) To remove your tag *and* remove this photo from Facebook, check I Want This Removed from Facebook, and then click Okay. You now see the Resolve a Problem panel.

(**5**) Check I'm In This Photo and I Don't Like It, and then click Continue.

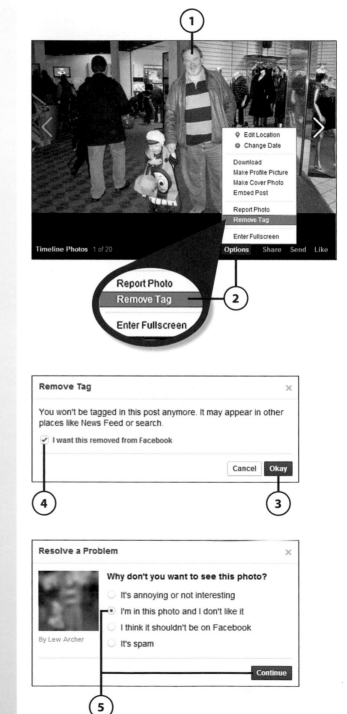

6 When Facebook asks why you don't like this photo, select from one of the reasons given: It's a bad photo of me, It's inappropriate, It makes me sad, It's embarrassing, or Other. Then click Continue.

7 Facebook now suggests you send a message to the original poster to remove this photo and displays a New Message panel. Accept the default message ("Hey, I don't like this photo. Take it down.") or enter your own personal message, and then click Send. The poster now has the option of removing the photo—or not. At this point, it's up to that person; Facebook does not remove photos on its own unless they're wildly inappropriate.

Resolve a Problem ✕

By Lew Archer

Why don't you like this photo?

○ It's a bad photo of me
○ It's inappropriate
○ It makes me sad
⦿ It's embarrassing
○ Other

Back Continue

6

New Message

The best way to remove this photo is to ask Lew to take it down. Your feedback may also help him post better pictures in the future.

To: Lew Archer

Message: Hey Lew, I don't like this photo. Take it down.

By Lew Archer

Tip: Write a note to Lew in your own words to help resolve the issue.

Send Cancel

7

Download a Photo

If you find a friend's photo that you really like, you can download it to your own computer, for your own personal use.

(1) Display the photo and mouse over the photo to display the menu at the bottom of the photo.

(2) Click Options, and then click Download.

(3) Click Save if you're prompted to open or save the file.

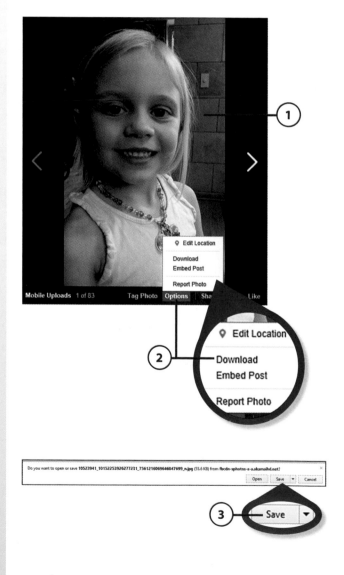

④ If you see the Save As dialog box, select where you want to save the file, and then click the Save button.

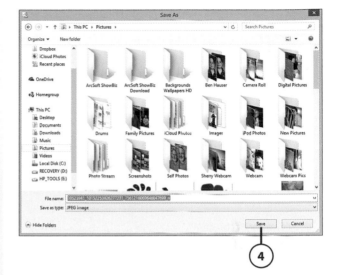

Print a Photo

Facebook does not have a "print" button for the photos on its site. You can, however, print a photo directly from its Facebook page, using the print feature in your web browser.

① Display and then right-click the photo to display a pop-up menu of options.

② Select Print or Print Picture.

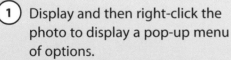

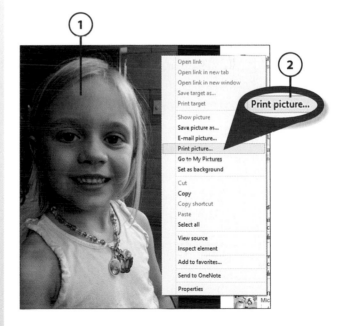

3 When the Print dialog box appears, select the printer you want to use.

4 Select how many copies you want to print.

5 Click the Print button.

Different Browsers

Your print options might be different depending on the web browser you're using. For example, Internet Explorer offers the Print Picture option from the pop-up menu. If you're using the Google Chrome browser, you have the Print option instead.

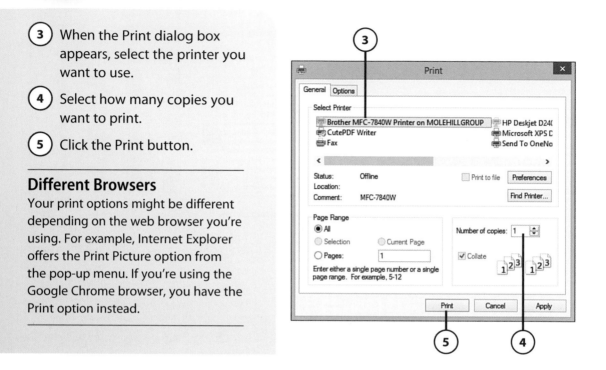

Sharing Your Photos with Friends

It seems like just about everybody these days has a digital camera, or a camera built into a smartphone or tablet. That means we're taking a lot more pictures than ever before—and those pictures can be shared with friends and family on Facebook.

The first thing you need to do is transfer your photos from your camera or phone to your computer. Then it's relatively easy to upload and share your own pictures on the Facebook site. You can upload new photos to an existing photo album or create a new album for newly uploaded photos.

>>>Go Further

POSTING PHOTOS FROM YOUR PHONE

If you use your cell phone to take photos, it's even easier to post those photos to Facebook. You don't have to transfer your phone photos to your computer first (although you can); Facebook lets you upload photos directly from your smartphone, using Facebook's mobile app.

With most smartphones today (including iPhone and Android phones), Facebook uploading is built into the phone's operating system. Just open your phone's photo gallery or app, and then open the photo you want to upload. Tap the Share icon, and then tap the Facebook icon. When prompted, enter some text to go along with the photo, add location information if you like, and select the privacy level for this post. When you're ready, tap the Post button. The selected photo is posted to your Facebook feed.

This mobile photo posting is explained in more detail in Chapter 20, "Using Facebook on Your iPhone, iPad, or Android Device." It's an easy way to share your photos as you take them.

Upload Photos to a New Photo Album

If you have a lot of photos to share on Facebook, the best approach is to create a series of virtual photo albums. This enables you to organize your photos by topic or date. For example, you might create an album for Summer Vacation, Thanksgiving 2014, Grandkids, or Retirement Party. Organizing your photos into albums also makes it easier for your friends to find specific photos.

① Click your name in the Facebook toolbar to display your Timeline page.

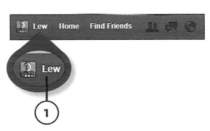

(2) Underneath the cover photo at the top of the page, click Photos to display your Photos page.

(3) Click the Create Album button to display the Open dialog box.

(4) Select the photo(s) you want to upload.

(5) Click the Open button to see the Untitled Album page.

Selecting Multiple Photos

You can upload more than one photo at a time. Hold down the Ctrl key while clicking files to select multiple files.

(6) Click Untitled Album and enter the desired album title.

(7) Click Say Something About This Album and enter an album description.

Optional Information

All the information you can add to a photo album is entirely optional; you can add as much or as little as you like. You don't even have to add a title—if you don't, Facebook uses the title Untitled Album.

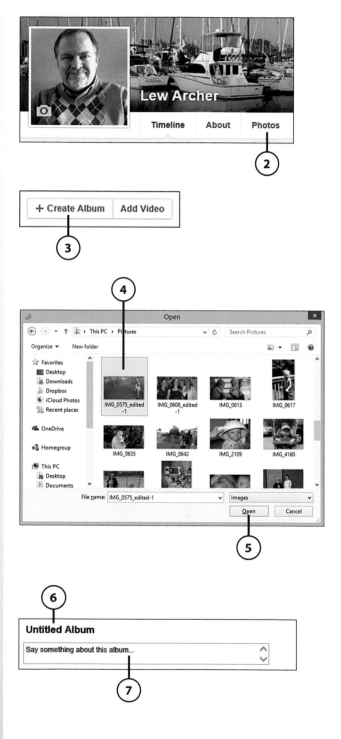

8 Enter a location in the Where Were These Taken? box to enter a geographic location for all the photos in this album. (You can later change the location for any specific photo, as noted in Step 13.)

9 Click Add Date and select a date from the pop-up box to add a date to all the photos in this album.

10 Click the Order by Date Taken button to display these photos in order of when they were taken.

11 To enter information about a specific picture, enter a description in the Say Something About This Photo box for that photo.

12 Click a photo's Date button and select the year, month, and date to enter the date the photo was taken.

13 If you want to enter a location for a specific photo that's different from the location you set for the entire album, click that photo's Location button and enter a location into the Where Was This? box to enter the place a photo was taken.

14 To tag a person in a given photo, click that person's face and enter his or her name when prompted.

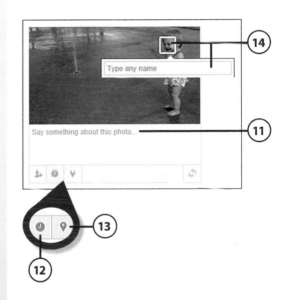

Photo Tagging

You identify people in your photos by *tagging* them—that is, you click a person in the photo, and then assign a friend's name to that part of the photo. You can then find photos where a given person appears by searching for that person's tag.

(15) Check the High Quality box at the bottom of the screen to upload these photos at a quality suitable for printing. Leave this box unchecked if the photos will only be viewed onscreen.

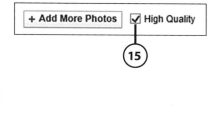

High-Quality Photos

For best possible picture quality for anyone downloading or printing your photos, check the High Quality option to upload and store your photos at their original resolution. Note, however, that it takes longer to upload high-quality photos than those in standard quality.

(16) Click the Privacy button and make a selection—Public, Friends, Only Me, or Custom—to determine who can view the photos in this album.

(17) Click the Post Photos button.

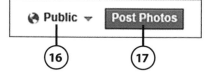

>>>*Go Further*
PHOTO REQUIREMENTS

You can post just about any kind of photo to your Facebook account. Facebook accepts photos in all popular file types, including JPG, PNG, GIF, TIFF, and BMP. Your picture files have to be no larger than 15MB in size and can't contain any adult or offensive content. You're also limited to uploading your own photos—that is, you can't copy and then upload photos from another person's website. Assuming your photos meet all these requirements, you're ready to upload.

Upload Photos to an Existing Photo Album

After you've created a photo album, you can easily upload more photos to that album.

1. Open your Timeline page, and then click Photos to display your Photos page.

2. Click Albums to display your existing photo albums.

3. Click the album you want to add new photos to.

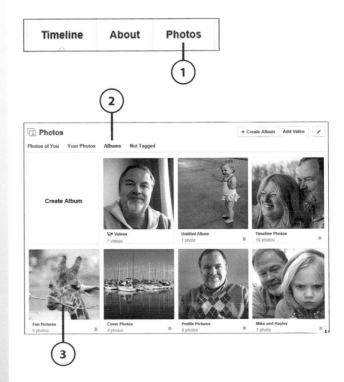

(4) When the album page opens, click the Add Photos button to display the Open dialog box.

(5) Navigate to and select the photo(s) to upload.

(6) Click the Open button.

(7) When the next page appears, you see the new photo(s) you've chosen to upload. Enter a description for each picture in the Say Something About This Photo box.

(8) To tag a person who appears in a photo, click that person's face and enter his or her name.

(9) Click that photo's Date button, and then select the year, month, and date to enter the date the photo was taken.

(10) Click that photo's Location button and then enter a location into the Where Was This? box to list the place the photo was taken.

Add Photos | Edit | Tag

④

⑤

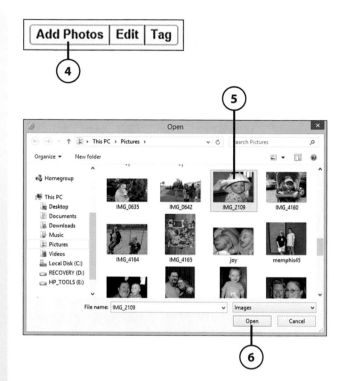

⑥

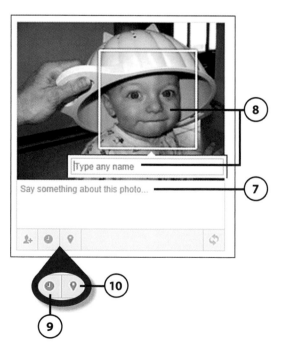

Type any name

Say something about this photo...   — ⑦

— ⑧

⑩

⑨

(**11**) Check the High Quality option to upload photos in the highest possible resolution.

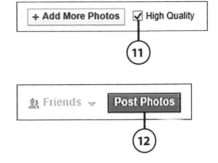

(**12**) Click the Post Photos button. The new photos are now added to the existing album.

Editing Your Photos and Albums

After you've created a new photo album and filled it with photos, you don't have to be done. You can, at any time, edit or delete individual photos and complete albums.

Edit a Photo's Description

You can, at any time, edit the description of a given photo.

(**1**) Click a picture to open that picture's photo viewer, and then click the Edit button to open the description panel.

2   Enter your description of the photo into the Add a Description box, or edit the existing description.

3   Enter the names of the people you were with into the Who Were You With? box.

4   Enter where the photo was taken into the Where Was This Photo Taken? box to add location information for the photo.

5   Use the year/month/date controls to change the date associated with this photo.

6   Click the Privacy button and make a new selection to change the privacy settings for this photo.

7   Click the Done Editing button when done.

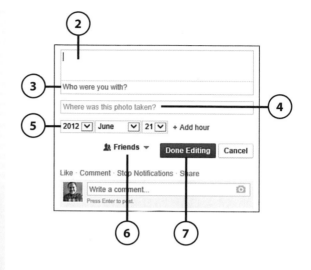

Edit a Photo Album

You can also edit the title, description, and other details of a Facebook photo album. You can change the location and date of the included photos, as well as revise the privacy level.

1   Open the photo album you want to edit and click the Edit button.

2 To change the album title, click the current title and make the appropriate edits.

3 To change the album description, click the current description (under the album title) and make the appropriate edits.

4 To change where these photos were taken, click the current location and enter a new location. (If no location was previously specified, enter a location into the Where Were These Taken? box.)

5 To change the privacy level of the album, click the Privacy button and make a new selection.

6 To change the date these photos were taken, click the Change Date button and select a new date from the pop-up box.

7 Click the Done button when finished.

2   3

Fun Pictures

Say something about this album...

♀ Where were these taken?

Album Contributors: [?]   Privacy:
Enter friends' names   👥 Friends ▾

4   5

Add Photos   Change Date   🗑   **Done**

6   7

Tag Friends in a Photo

You can, at any time, "tag" friends who appear in the photos you upload. You don't need their permission to do so, either. This makes it easy for your friends to view themselves and other friends in your photos.

Multiple Tags

You can tag multiple people in each photo. For example, if you have a photo of you and a good friend, you can tag both yourself and your friend. This photo appears in your own photo albums, of course, but it also shows up on your friend's Photos page, in the Photos and Videos of section.

(1) Display the photo you want to tag, and then click the Tag Photo button to the right of the photo.

(2) Click the face of the person you want to tag. Facebook displays a box around the selected person, along with a list of suggested friends.

(3) If the person's name is in this list, click it.

(4) If the person's name isn't on the list, begin typing the name of the person into the text box, and then select the person's name from the resulting list.

(5) Click the Done Tagging button.

Face Recognition

Facebook employs face-recognition technology that attempts to automatically figure out which friends are in your pictures; if Facebook recognizes a face, it suggests a friend's name for tagging. The goal is to make tagging pictures easier, so that more people do it.

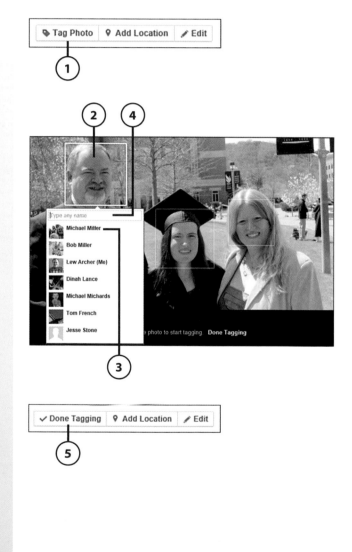

Delete a Photo

If you later discover that you've uploaded a photo you don't want to share, Facebook lets you delete individual photos within an album.

1. Display the photo you want to delete, and then mouse over the photo to display the bottom menu.

2. Click Options to display the pop-up menu.

3. Click Delete This Photo

4. Click Confirm in the Delete Photo panel.

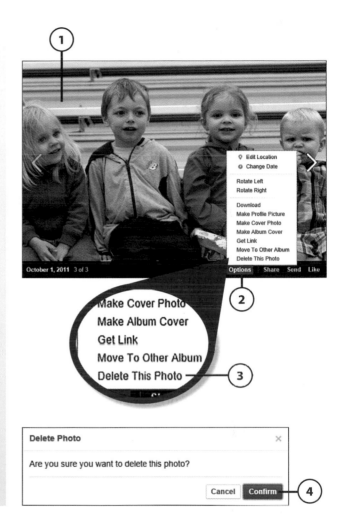

It's Not All Good

Deletion Is Final

When you delete a photo on Facebook, there's no way of undeleting that photo. You can, however, re-upload the photo to the album from scratch.

When you delete a photo album, not only is the deletion final, but you also delete all the photos within that album. Make sure you really want to delete a photo or album before you proceed.

Delete a Photo Album

You're not limited to deleting single photos. You can also delete complete photo albums—and all the photos within.

(1) Open the album you want to delete and click the Manage button.

(2) Click the Delete Album (trash can) button.

(3) Click the Delete Album button in the Delete Album? panel.

| + Create Album | Add Video | ✏ |—(1)

| Add Photos | Change Date | 🗑 | **Done** |
(2)

Delete Album?   ✕

Are you sure you want to delete Fun Pictures? Photos in this album
will also be deleted.

Cancel   **Delete Album**
(3)

Video player

Video description

Playback controls

In this chapter, you find out how to share your favorite home movies and videos with your Facebook friends.

→ Viewing Videos from Friends
→ Sharing Your Own Videos on Facebook
→ Sharing YouTube Videos on Facebook

Viewing and Sharing Home Movies

Just as many people use Facebook to view and share family photos, Facebook is also a convenient way to view and share home movies and other videos. You can upload any videos you've taken with your camcorder, digital camera, tablet, or smartphone, and your friends and family members can view them from the comfort of their computer screens.

And you can view your friends' videos, as well; playback is just a click away. It's a far sight easier than setting up the old 8mm projector and screen in your living room, or even trading VHS tapes!

Viewing Videos from Friends

If your friends or family members have a home movie they'd like you to watch, Facebook is the place to share it. You can upload to Facebook just about any type of video, where you (and other friends) can watch it on your computer. In fact, if you access Facebook from your smartphone or tablet, you can even watch these home movies in the palm of your hand.

View an Uploaded Video

When one of your friends uploads a video to Facebook, it shows up in your News Feed as a thumbnail image with a playback arrow on top. Playing a video is as easy as clicking that image.

(1) Navigate to the status update that contains the video, and click the video thumbnail to play the video. (In some cases, the video plays automatically when you scroll to the post, but without sound—kind of like a muted preview. You need to click the video to play it back with sound.)

YouTube Videos

If someone has posted a video from YouTube, Vimeo, or another video sharing site, playback will probably take place within the News Feed. To view the video on the YouTube or Vimeo site, click the title of the video to open that site in a new tab in your web browser.

2 In some cases, video playback begins in the News Feed itself. In other cases, playback begins in a separate video player similar to Facebook's photo lightbox. If playback is in the News Feed, but you want to view the video at a larger size, mouse over the video to display the playback controls at the bottom and click the Full Screen icon. Click Esc on your computer keyboard to return to normal playback mode.

3 To pause the playback, mouse over the video to display the playback controls, and then click the Pause button; the button changes to a Play button. Click the Play button to resume playback.

4 Click and drag the volume control to raise or lower the playback volume.

5 Click and drag the time slider to move to another point in the video.

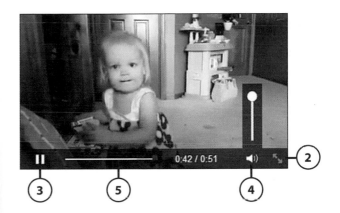

Time and HD

The elapsed and total time of the video is displayed to the right of the time slider in the playback controls. If a video was recorded and uploaded in high definition, you see an HD button; click this to view the video in high def.

Comment On and Like a Friend's Video

Just as you can comment on your friends' status updates, you can also comment on any video they upload. All comments are displayed beneath the video in the News Feed.

(1) Click the Like link beneath the video player to like the video.

(2) Click the Comment link beneath the video player to comment on the video. This expands the Comment box.

(3) Type your comments into the Comment box; press Enter when done.

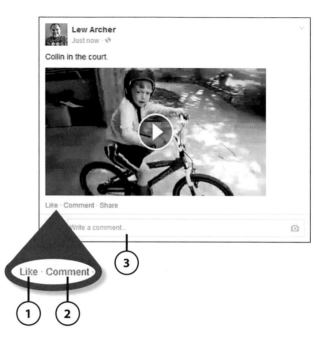

View All of a Friend's Videos

All the videos a friend has uploaded are displayed in a Videos album on the friend's Photos page. You can play back any video from here.

(1) Go to your friend's Timeline page and click the Photos button underneath the cover image to display your friend's Photos page.

(2) Click Albums to display your friend's photo albums.

(3) Click the Videos album to display all this person's videos.

Upload Order

The videos in the Videos album are organized by date uploaded. Newest uploads are displayed first.

(4) Click a video thumbnail to play that video.

(5) Playback begins in a video player similar to Facebook's photo lightbox. To display playback controls, mouse over the video.

(6) Click the Pause button to pause playback; the button changes to a Play button. Click the Play button to resume playback.

(7) Click and drag the volume control to raise or lower the playback volume.

(8) Click and drag the time slider to move to another point in the video.

(9) For those videos that were recorded and uploaded in high definition (HD), click the HD button to view the video in high def.

(10) Click the Fullscreen button to display the video on your full computer screen. Press Esc on your computer keyboard to return to the video playback page.

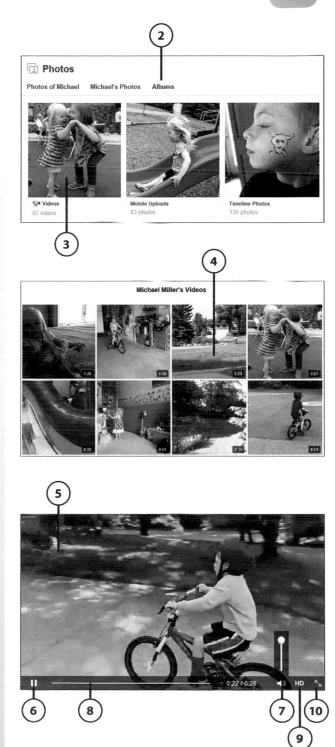

Close the Video Player

To close the video player, click the X in the upper-right corner above the description.

Sharing Your Own Videos on Facebook

If you shoot your own home videos, you can share them with friends and family by uploading them to Facebook. Facebook lets you upload videos already stored as digital files or create new videos in real time from your computer's webcam.

>>>Go Further
VIDEO EDITING AND UPLOADS

When uploading videos to Facebook, the video files must be no more than 20 minutes long and no more than 1024MB (approximately 1GB) in size. Facebook accepts videos in all major video file formats, including high-definition videos.

You might want to edit your videos before you upload them, to cut out dead spots and string together multiple clips. You can do this on your computer, using a video-editing software program. The most popular programs include Adobe Premiere Elements (www.adobe.com/products/premiereel/, $99.99), Pinnacle Studio HD (www.pinnaclesys.com, $59.95), and Sony Vegas Movie Studio HD (www.sonycreativesoftware.com/moviestudiohd/, $49.95). All produce files that you can upload to your Facebook account.

Upload a Video File

Facebook lets you upload just about any type of video and share it as a status update, which means all your friends should see it as part of their News Feeds. Your uploaded videos also end up in the Videos album on your Photos page, accessible from your Timeline for all your friends to view.

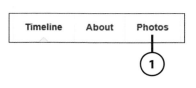

(1) Open your Timeline page and click Photos to open your Photos page.

2 Click the Add Video button to display the Upload Video panel.

3 Click the Choose File button to display the Choose File to Upload or Open dialog box.

4 Navigate to and select the video file you want to upload.

5 Click the Open button to return to the Upload Video panel.

6 Enter a title for this video into the Title box.

7 Enter a short description of the video into the Description box.

8 Enter a location in the Where box to specify where the video was taken.

9 Click the Privacy button and select who can view this video: Public, Friends, Only Me, or Custom.

10 Click the Post button when done.

Processing

After a video is uploaded, Facebook must process it into the proper format to distribute on its site. This might take several minutes. You should be informed when the processing is complete; you can then edit the video description if you like, or select a thumbnail image for the video.

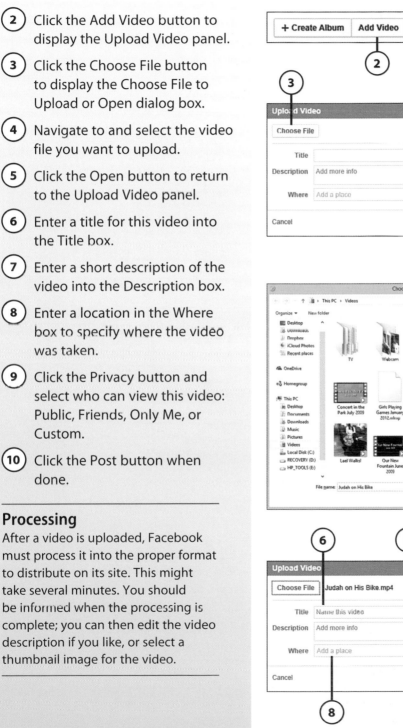

Edit Video Information

You can enter or edit information about any video you've uploaded at any time. You can also tag friends appearing in a video, as well as select a thumbnail image for the video.

(1) From your Photos page, display all your albums and then click to open the Videos album.

(2) Mouse over the video and click Edit or Remove to display the pop-up menu.

(3) Click Edit This Video to display the Edit Video page.

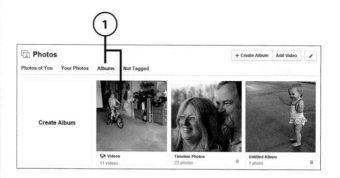

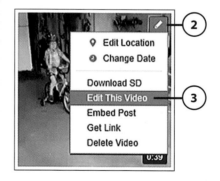

4 To "tag" a person appearing in the video, enter his or her name into the In This Video box. To remove a person previously tagged, click the X next to his or her name.

5 Go to the Title box and make any necessary changes to the video's title.

6 Go to the Where section and enter a location to add location information for the video.

7 To add information about when the video was recorded, go to the When section and click Add Year, then select a year. Click Add Month, then select a month. Click Add Day and select a day.

8 Go to the Description box and make any necessary changes to the video's description.

9 Click the Privacy button and make a new selection to change who can view this video.

10 For longer videos, you can select from up to ten different thumbnail images for the video. Click the left and right arrows in the Choose a Thumbnail to select a thumbnail image.

11 Click the Save button when you're done making changes.

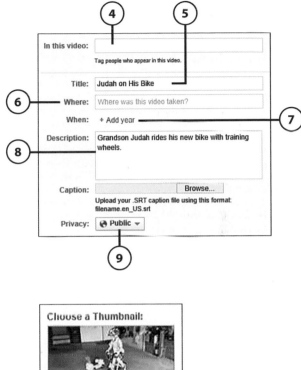

Delete a Video

Ever upload a video you later decided you really don't want anybody else to watch? Fortunately, Facebook enables you to delete any video you've previously uploaded.

 From your Photos page, display all your albums and then click to open the Videos album.

② Mouse over the video, and click Edit or Remove to display the pop-up menu.

③ Click Delete Video.

④ Click the Confirm button in the Delete Video dialog box.

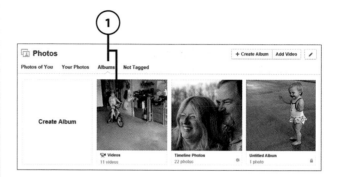

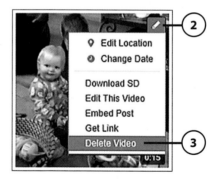

Sharing YouTube Videos on Facebook

YouTube (www.youtube.com) is the world's largest online video community, with hundreds of millions of videos available for viewing. Many Facebook users like to share videos from the YouTube site with their Facebook friends. YouTube makes it easy to do this.

YouTube Account

To share YouTube videos, you first must have either a YouTube or Google account. Both are free.

Share a YouTube Video

You can share videos you've uploaded yourself to YouTube.

1 Use your web browser to go to YouTube (www.youtube.com) and log in to your YouTube account.

2 Navigate to the video you want to post to Facebook.

3 Click Share beneath the video player to expand the Share panel.

4 Click the Facebook button to open the Post to Facebook window.

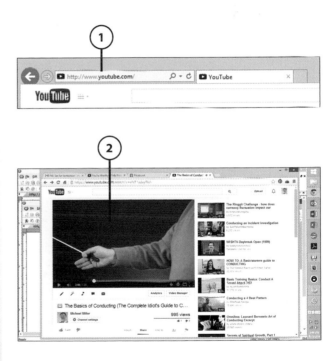

5 Enter an accompanying message into the Say Something About This box.

6 Click the Privacy button to determine who can view this video.

7 Click the Share button. The video is posted as a status update to your Facebook timeline.

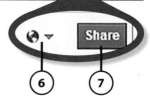

Linking Accounts

The first time you try to share a YouTube video on Facebook, you see the Facebook Login window. Enter your email address and Facebook password, and then click the Login button. (You won't see this window after this first time.)

View a Shared YouTube Video

When one of your friends shares a YouTube video, it appears as a status update in your News Feed. You can view the YouTube video directly within your News Feed.

1 Go to the status update that includes the YouTube video and then click the thumbnail image to begin playback.

2 Mouse over the video to display the playback controls.

3 Click the Pause button to pause playback; click the Play button to resume playback.

4 To view the video on the YouTube site, click the YouTube icon.

Lew Archer
3 mins · YouTube · 🌐 ▾

Here's a great video that shows you how to conduct music!

The Basics of Conducting (The Complete Idiot's Guide to Conducting Music Lesson 1)
Lesson 1 from The Complete Idiot's Guide to Conducting Music by author Michael Miller: The...

WWW.YOUTUBE.COM

Like · Comment · Share · Subscribe on YouTube

👍 Michael Miller likes this.

Write a comment...
Press Enter to post.

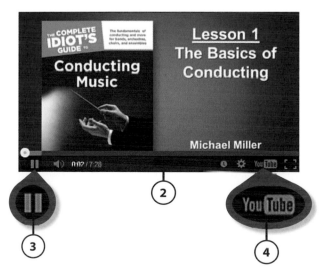

Profile picture   Cover image   Timeline

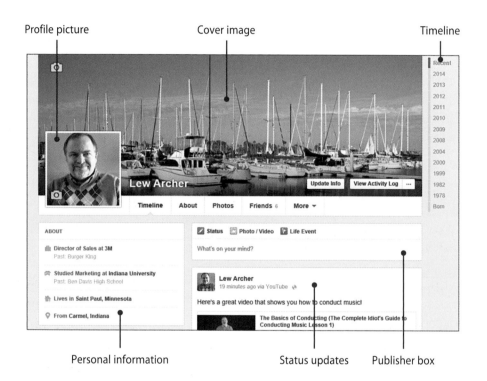

Personal information   Status updates   Publisher box

In this chapter, you find out how to personalize your Facebook Timeline page.

→ Changing the Look and Feel of Your Timeline
→ Editing the Contents of Your Timeline

9

Personalizing Your Profile and Timeline

When old friends want to see what you've been up to all these years, they turn to a single Facebook page—your personal Timeline. Your Timeline page hosts all your personal information and status updates, so that friends and family can learn all about you at a glance. Fortunately, you have some control over what gets displayed on your Timeline—it's your personal page on the Facebook site.

Changing the Look and Feel of Your Timeline

All your personal information, including the status updates you've posted, are displayed on your Facebook Timeline page. Your Timeline is essentially your home base on Facebook, the place where all your Facebook friends can view your information and activity.

You access your own Timeline page by clicking your name on the Facebook toolbar. From there, you can customize (to a degree) how your Timeline looks, and what information it contains.

Change Your Profile Picture

Your Timeline page includes your account's profile picture—and this is the first thing many people change. Your profile picture is an image of your choosing (it can be a picture of you or of anything, really) that appears not only on your Timeline page, but also accompanies every post you make on the Facebook site. (For example, your profile picture appears in your friends' News Feeds, alongside each of your status updates.)

You can easily change the image that appears as your profile picture. Some users change this image frequently; others find a photo they like and stick to it.

1. Click your name in the toolbar (or your picture in the sidebar menu) to display your Timeline page.

2. Mouse over your profile picture and click Update Profile Picture to display the Update Profile Picture panel. (If this is the first time adding a profile picture, click the Add Profile Picture button instead.)

3. Select Upload Photo to display the Choose File to Upload or Open dialog box if you're uploading a photo from your computer. (Skip to step 6 if you instead want to take a photo with your webcam.)

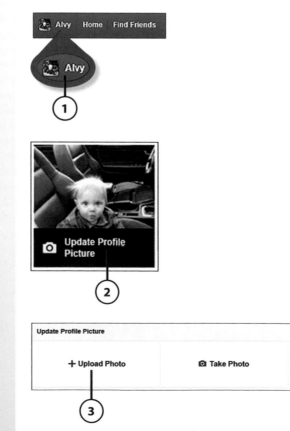

4 Navigate to and select the photo you want to use.

5 Click the Open button.

6 You can also shoot a new profile picture using your computer's webcam. From the Update Profile Picture pane, click Take Photo to display the Take a Profile Picture panel.

7 Smile and click the Take button; this initiates a 3-2-1 countdown before the picture is taken.

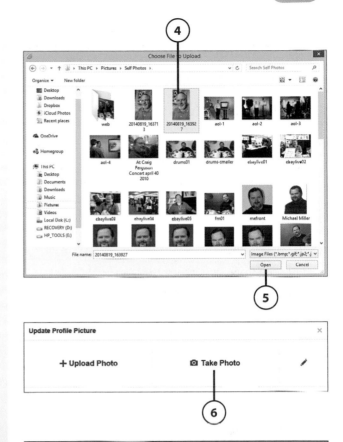

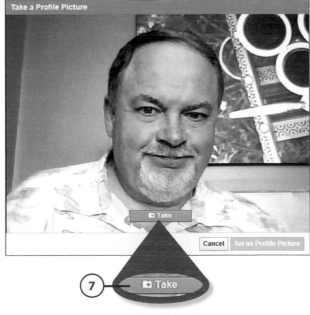

(8) Click the Set as Profile Picture button.

Edit Your Picture Thumbnail

In many instances, the photo you choose for your profile picture isn't framed correctly for use as your thumbnail image. You can, however, recrop the image to better fit the thumbnail dimensions.

(1) From your Timeline page, mouse over your profile photo and select Update Profile Picture to display the Update Profile Picture panel.

(2) Click the Edit Thumbnail icon to display the Edit Thumbnail panel.

(3) Use your mouse to drag the thumbnail image until it looks like you want it to look.

(4) Click the Save Profile Picture button.

Add a Cover Image

By default, your profile picture appears against a shaded background at the top of your Timeline page—not very visually interesting. You can, however, select a background image (called a *cover image*) to appear on the top of the page. Many people choose landscapes or other artistic images that provide an interesting but non-obtrusive background to their profile picture; others choose more personal photos as their covers.

Cover Image Specs

Your cover image should be wider than it is tall. The ideal size is 851 pixels wide by 315 pixels tall—although if you upload a smaller image, Facebook stretches it to fill the space.

(**1**) To add your first cover image, go to your Timeline page and click the Add Cover Photo button. A pop-up menu with several options displays.

Change an Existing Cover

To change an existing cover image, mouse over the image, click the Change Cover button, and then make an appropriate selection.

(**2**) To select from a photo already uploaded to Facebook, click Choose from My Photos to display the Choose from My Photos panel.

(**3**) Click one of the photos you see, or click Photo Albums to select a photo from one of your photo albums.

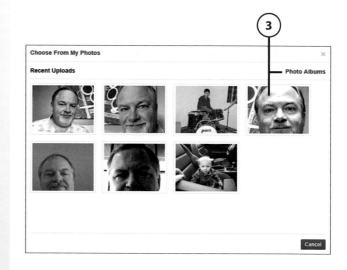

(**4**) To select a photo stored on your computer, click the Add Cover Photo button, and then click the Upload Photo option to display the Choose File to Upload or Open dialog box.

5 Navigate to and select the picture you want to use.

6 Click the Open button.

7 You're prompted to reposition the cover image by dragging it around the cover image space. Use your mouse to reposition the image as necessary.

8 Click the Save Changes button.

Reposition Your Cover Image

You can reposition the picture used as your cover image at any time. Mouse over your cover image, click Change Cover, and then click Reposition. Use your mouse to position the image as you wish, and then click the Save Changes button.

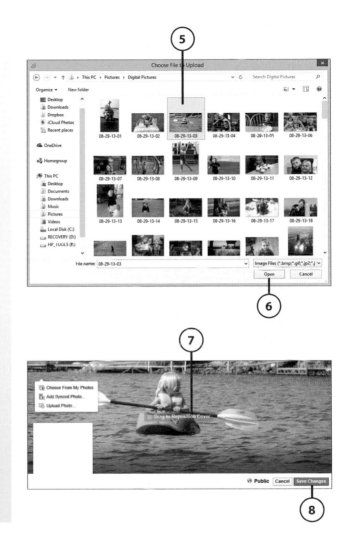

Editing the Contents of Your Timeline

Beneath the cover image on your Timeline page are buttons that lead to additional information and content, such as your friends list and photos you've uploaded. You can't change these buttons; they are what they are.

Scroll down and you see your Timeline proper, in two-column format. The left column contains personal information about you, in various themed boxes—About, Photos, Friends, Places, and the like. The right column contains all the status updates and other Facebook activities in which you've participated, in reverse chronological order (newest first, in other words).

You can edit most of the personal information displayed on your Timeline page, to either add new events or hide information you'd rather not leave public. You can also choose to hide unwanted status updates, or highlight those updates that are more important to you.

Hide and Delete Status Updates

The main section of your Timeline displays all the status updates you've made on Facebook, from the first day you signed up to just now. You don't have to display every single status update, however; if there's an embarrassing update out there, you can choose to either hide it from view or completely delete it.

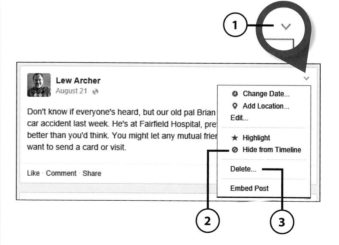

(1) Go to your Timeline page, mouse over the status update, and then click the down arrow in the top-right corner to display a menu of options.

(2) Click Hide from Timeline to hide this update but not permanently delete it. (Hidden posts can be unhidden in the future.)

(3) Click Delete (or, if it's a photo you've posted, Delete Photo) to permanently delete this update from Facebook. (Deleted posts cannot be undeleted.)

Not Everything Can Be Deleted

Not all status updates can be deleted. If the Delete option doesn't appear, you should opt to hide the update instead.

Highlight Your Favorite Status Updates

You can draw attention to your favorite or most important status updates by highlighting them on your Timeline. A highlighted post appears with a blue banner at the top-right corner.

(**1**) Go to your Timeline page, mouse over the status update you want to highlight, and click the down arrow to display a menu of options.

(**2**) Click Highlight.

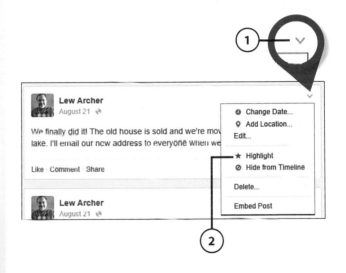

Unhighlight a Post

If you change your mind about what's important, you can "unhighlight" a previously highlighted post. Just return to the post on your Timeline, click the down arrow, and then click Remove from Highlights.

View and Edit Your Facebook Activity

Your Timeline page presents all your Facebook activity in a nice, visually attractive fashion. However, if you want a more straightforward view of what you've done online, you can display and edit your Activity Log. This is a chronological list of everything you've done on the Facebook site, from status updates to links to comments you've made on others' posts.

>>>*Go Further*
CLEAN UP YOUR TIMELINE

Many users find the Activity Log the most efficient way to clean up entries on their Timelines. It's easier to see what's posted (and available to post) from the more condensed Activity Log listing than it is by scrolling through the entire Timeline.

1. From your Timeline page, click the View Activity Log button at the bottom-right corner of the cover image. This displays your Facebook Activity Log.

2. Click the Allowed on Timeline (pencil) button for an item, and then click Hidden from Timeline to hide that item from your Timeline.

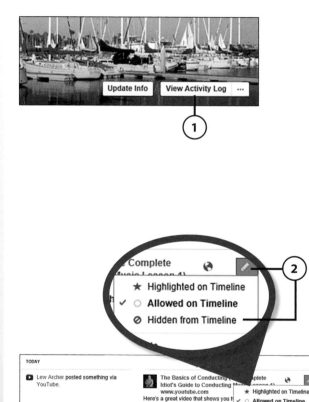

3 Click the Hidden from Timeline button for a hidden item, and then click Allowed on Timeline to redisplay a hidden item on your Timeline.

4 To change who can view an item, click the Privacy button and select Public, Friends, Only Me, or Custom.

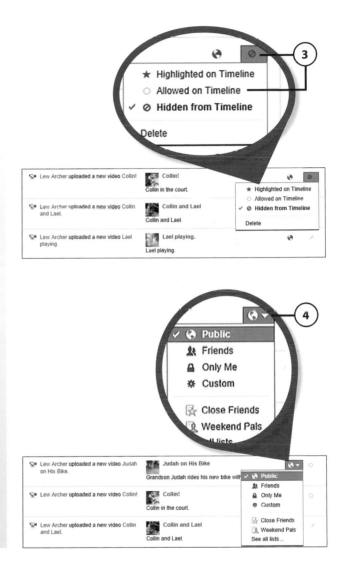

Update Your Profile Information

Many people don't fully complete their profiles when first joining Facebook. Maybe you forgot to include certain information, or maybe you entered it wrong. In any case, Facebook lets you easily edit or update the personal information in your Facebook profile. You can also select who can view what information.

>>>Go Further

THE MORE FACEBOOK KNOWS…

All the personal information that Facebook requests of you is optional—you don't have to enter it if you don't want to. For security reasons, you might share less. On the other hand, the more Facebook knows about you, the better it can suggest appropriate activities and match you with potential friends. For example, Facebook makes more and more relevant friend suggestions when you add every school you've attended and every employer you've worked for. So enter as much information as you're comfortable with, and let it go at that.

1 Go to your Timeline page and click the Update Info button at the lower-right corner of your cover image.

2 This displays a special version of your About page, designed for the entry of new information. The Overview section is selected by default in the left-hand column; click whichever type of information in the left column you want to edit.

3 Click any item you want to add, such as Add a Workplace or Add a School.

Update Info   View Activity Log   …

About

Overview
Work and Education
Places You've Lived
Contact and Basic Info
Family and Relationships
Details About You

+ Add a workplace
+ Add a school
+ Add your current city
+ Add your hometown
1 family member

alvy.singer.982@facebook.com
June 23, 1990

4 You now see a series of boxes you can fill in for specific information. Enter the information as requested.

5 Click the Privacy button for this item, and then select who can view this information—Public, Friends, Only Me, or Custom.

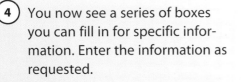

Only Me

Selecting the Only Me option makes that piece of information visible only to yourself. No one else on Facebook, not even your friends, can see it.

6 Click Save Changes to close editing on this item.

7 To edit another section of your profile, repeat steps 3 through 6.

>>>Go Further

WHO KNOWS WHAT?

Not everyone viewing your profile needs to see all your information. For example, you might want everyone to view your birthdate, but not necessarily the year of your birth. You might want only your friends to view your relationship status, or you might not want to share your personal contact information with anyone. You can fine-tune your profile as granularly as you like, in this fashion, to create a clear division between your public and private lives.

Add a Life Event

Facebook's intention with the Timeline is to tell the "story of your life" on a single page. (In fact, Facebook calls the status updates you post "stories.") But Facebook can display only those events it knows about based on what you've entered into your personal profile. You can, however, supplement this information by adding other milestones—what Facebook calls *life events*—to your Timeline.

(1) On your Timeline page, go to the Publisher box and click Life Event. This expands the Publisher box to include a list of different types of events.

(2) Click the type of event you want to add—Work & Education, Family & Relationships, Home & Living, Health & Wellness, or Travel & Experiences.

(3) Facebook displays options for the type of event you selected. The options available differ by the type of event; select the option that best applies to the event you want to add, or select Create Your Own to add anything not listed here.

Status   Photo / Video   Life Event

- Work & Education
- Family & Relationships
- Home & Living
- Health & Wellness
- Travel & Experiences

Status   Photo / Video   Life Event

- Work & Education
- Family & Relationships
- Home & Living
- Health & Wellness
- Travel & Experiences

Moved...
Bought a Home...
Home Improvement...
New Roommate...

New Vehicle...

Create Your Own...

4 You now see a panel specific to the type of event you selected. For example, if you opt to enter that you've moved, you see the Moved panel, with fields such as Where To, From, and With. Enter the appropriate information for this event.

5 In many instances, there is the opportunity to add photos related to the event. Click Upload Photos to choose pictures stored on your computer, or Choose from Photos to select pictures previously uploaded to a Facebook photo album.

6 To determine who can view this event, click the Privacy button and select from the available options—Public, Friends, Only Me, and Custom.

7 Click the Save button. The new event is posted to your Timeline.

>>>Go Further
LIFE EVENTS

You can add to your Facebook Timeline just about any life event that's important to you, such as moving into a new house, changing jobs, or welcoming a new grandchild. This lets you document major events in your life, and also lets your Facebook friends travel back in time to view what you've done in the past.

That said, you should always use discretion when adding life events to your Timeline. For example, do you really want your kids and grandkids knowing when you took your first drink, or your spouse knowing every intimate relationship you had before you got married? Use your own best judgment, but err on the side of being discreet.

Unread
message

Messages
button

Click to view all
private messages

Click to send
a new message

In this chapter, you find out how to send and receive private messages to and from other Facebook users.

Exchanging Private Messages

Facebook is a public social network, which means it encourages public interaction between you and your friends. But you might not want all your communication to be public; sometimes you just want to send a private message to someone you know.

That's why, in addition to its public status updates, Facebook includes a private messaging feature for its members. It's kind of like sending an email to a friend or family member—but without having to access your email program or service.

Sending Private Messages

Facebook lets any user send private messages to any other user. These messages do not appear on either person's News Feed or Timeline page; it's the Facebook equivalent of private email.

Send a Private Message

Sending a private message to another Facebook user is as easy as sending an email to that person—even easier, actually. Your master Facebook friends list functions much as a contacts list in an email program; you can add recipients to a message just by typing a few letters of their name.

1. Click Messages in the navigation sidebar to display the Messages page.

2. Click the New Message button to display the New Message pane.

3. Enter the name of the recipient into the To box.

4. As you type, Facebook displays matching friends; select the desired recipient from the list.

5. Enter your message into the Write a Message box.

6. Press Enter or click the Send button to send the message on its way.

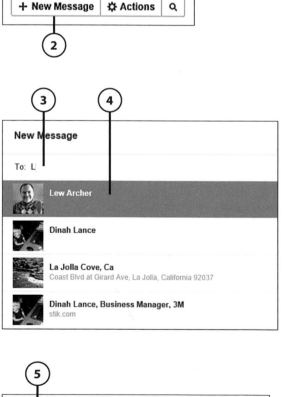

Share a Photo via Private Message

Facebook's private messages are quite similar to traditional emails. Just as you can attach photos to your email messages, you can also include photos in your Facebook private messages. This is a great way to privately share those family photos you've uploaded to Facebook—without making them public for all of Facebook to see.

1. Open a new private message as described in the "Send a Private Message" task.

2. Click Add Photos to open the Choose File to Upload or Open dialog box.

3. Navigate and select the picture you want to attach.

4. Click the Open button.

5. Complete your message and click the Send button.

Photos and Videos

You can also send videos via Facebook private message. Follow these same steps, but select a video file instead of an image file.

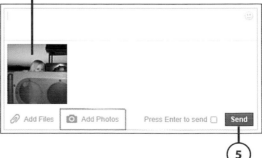

Attached photo

Attach a File to a Message

You can also use Facebook's private message system to send other types of files to your Facebook friends. For example, you might want to send a Word document file to someone you work with on community projects, or an Excel spreadsheet file to your accountant or financial advisor.

1. Open a new private message as described in the "Send a Private Message" task.

2. Click Add Files to open the Choose File to Upload or Open dialog box.

3. Navigate to and select the file you want to attach.

4. Click the Open button.

5. Complete your message and click the Send button.

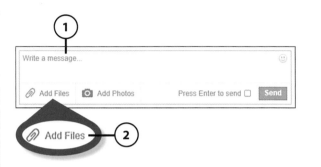

Attached file

Viewing Private Messages

When you receive a new private message from a friend, you see a red number on top of the Messages button on the Facebook toolbar. Click the Messages button to read all your new private messages. Better yet, open the separate Messages page to view all your private messages—new and old.

Read a Message

Facebook's Messages page serves as your inbox for all messages sent to you from across the Facebook site, including private messages, email messages, chat (instant) messages, and even text messages sent via mobile phone. To Facebook, one type of message is just like another; it really doesn't distinguish between the different types of messages.

Message Types

To see what type of message you've received on the Messages page, look for the icon displayed next to each message, beside the time/date indicator. An envelope icon indicates an email message; a word balloon icon indicates a chat or instant message; a phone icon indicates a text message; and no icon means you got a private message from a Facebook friend.

---

1. Click the Messages button in the Facebook toolbar to view your most recent messages.

2. Click any message snippet to view the entire message in a separate message pane.

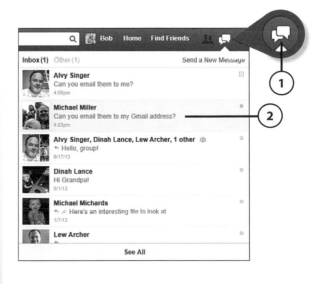

③ All your messages to and from this person are displayed in the form of a flowing conversation. The newest messages are at the bottom of the pane.

④ To respond to this person's latest message, enter your message into the bottom text box and press Enter.

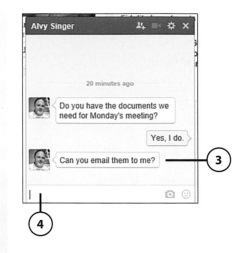

Live Chat

If the person you're messaging is online at the same time you are, your private messages become a live text chat. Learn more in Chapter 11, "Chatting with Friends and Family in Real Time."

View All Messages

Clicking the Messages button on the toolbar only displays your most recent messages. You can view all messages you've received on the Messages page.

① On the Facebook toolbar, click the Messages button to display the menu of messages and options.

② At the bottom of the menu, click See All to open the Messages panel.

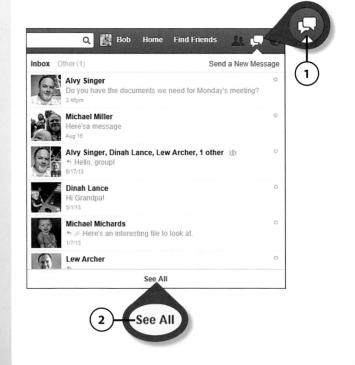

3 All messages are listed in a scrolling list on the left side of the page. Click a message to view all messages to and from that person in the center section of the page.

4 To reply to the current message, enter your text into the Write a Reply box at the bottom of the page, and then click the Reply button.

NON-MEMBER MESSAGES

The Inbox on the Messages page displays only messages from your Facebook friends, not messages sent from other Facebook members or those sent via email from outsiders. To view these non-friend messages, click Other at the top of the sidebar.

You

Person you're
chatting with

Click to
close chat

Select your
webcam

Select your
microphone

In this chapter, you find out how to conduct one-on-one text and video chats with your Facebook friends.

→ Text Chatting on Facebook
→ Video Chatting on Facebook

11

Chatting with Friends and Family in Real Time

If you have far-flung relatives and friends, are a snowbird, or travel a lot, you know how hard it is to spend long times away from the people you love. Exchanging the occasional email is fine, but it's not quite the same as being there.

Facebook has a solution to this problem—two solutions, actually. First, you can do online text messaging—what Facebook calls *chat*—with anyone on your Facebook friends list. And if that's not good enough, you can conduct face-to-face video chats with distant friends and family, using your computer screen and webcam. It's just like being there—and it's all free!

Text Chatting on Facebook

What Facebook calls *chat* is really a form of online instant messaging, which is kind of like text messaging, but on your computer instead of your phone. With Facebook chat, you can carry on real-time text conversations with other Facebook members using the Facebook website.

Interestingly, Facebook's text chat is an extension of the private messages covered in Chapter 10, "Exchanging Private Messages." If you send a private message to someone who's currently online, it turns into a text chat session. If you try to text chat with someone who's not currently online, it gets sent as a private message. It's really two sides of the same coin.

Start a Chat Session

You can start a chat session with any of your Facebook friends who are also online and willing to spend a few minutes texting with you. It's a great way to go one-on-one with the people you love.

(1) Click the Chat gadget at the bottom-right corner of any Facebook page to display the full Chat panel.

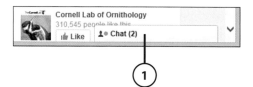

Wide Displays

If your web browser is wide enough, Facebook might display the Chat panel as part of the sidebar menu. If so, you'll see the list of online friends at the lower left of the page, underneath the other sidebar menu items.

2 Friends who are online and ready to chat are identified with a round green icon, whether they're connecting via the web or a mobile device. Click the name of the friend you want to chat with to open an individual Chat panel with the selected friend.

3 Type a text message in the bottom text box and press Enter.

4 Your messages, along with your friend's responses, appear in consecutive order within the Chat panel. Continue typing new messages as you want.

5 To end the chat session and close the Chat panel, click the X at the top right of the panel.

Respond to a Chat Invitation

You can initiate a chat session with a friend, or a friend can invite you to chat. Responding to a chat invitation is as easy as typing on your computer keyboard.

(1) When another user invites you to chat, you hear a short sound and see a new Chat panel for that person open on your Facebook page.

(2) Start typing to reply to your friend's initial message. Your conversation appears in the body of the Chat panel.

(3) To end the chat session, click the X at the top of the Chat panel.

Add More Friends to a Chat

Chatting isn't limited to a one-on-one conversation. On Facebook, more than two people can chat at a time in a group chat. This is great for exchanging messages between groups of friends or co-workers who are interested in the same topic.

1. Start a chat with another person. From that Chat panel, click the Add More Friends to Chat button.

2. You now see an Add Friends to Chat box near the top of the Chat panel. Enter the name of a friend you'd like to add to the chat; as you type, a list of matching friends is displayed.

3. Click to select the friend you want to add to the chat.

4. Repeat steps 2 and 3 to add other friends to this chat, and then click the Done button.

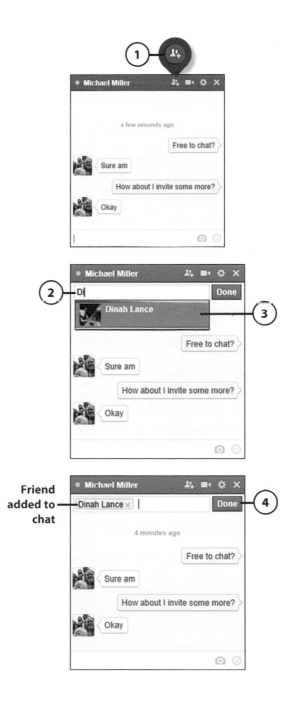

Friend added to chat

(5) A new Chat panel for the group chat now appears. Your messages, along with your friends' responses, appear in consecutive order within the Chat panel. Type your messages into the bottom text box and press Enter to send them to the group.

(6) To end the chat session and close the Chat panel, click the X at the top right of the panel.

> >>>*Go Further*
> ## DISABLING CHAT
>
> If you'd rather not be available for online chats, you can turn off Facebook chat. Open the main Chat panel, click the Options (gear) button, and then click Turn Off Chat. To turn Chat back on, repeat this process and click Turn On Chat instead.
>
> You can also choose to "hide" from certain friends in chat by clicking the Options button and then clicking Advanced. When the Advanced Chat Settings dialog box appears, check Turn On Chat for All Friends Except and then enter the names of those friends you don't want to chat with.
>
> Likewise, you can choose to enable chat only for certain friends. Open the Advanced Chat Settings dialog box, check Turn On Chat for Only Some Friends, and then enter the names of selected friends.

Video Chatting on Facebook

If you have a webcam built into or attached to your computer, you can talk to other Facebook users face-to-face using Facebook's video chat feature. Video chatting is a great way to get up-close and personal with distant family and friends; you can see them and they can see you.

Skype

Facebook's video chat feature is powered by Skype, one of the more popular Internet-based voice and video communication services. In fact, you can connect your Facebook and Skype accounts, so that your Facebook friends appear as Skype contacts.

Start a Video Chat

You can establish a video chat with any of your Facebook friends who have a working webcam on their computers. The friend you want to talk to also has to be online at the same time you are, and then you can fire up your webcams and start talking.

Install the Chat Applet

The first time you use Facebook's video chat, you are prompted to download and install the necessary background chat applet on your computer. (An applet is a small application that runs in the background—in this case, to enable video chat.) Follow the onscreen instructions to do so.

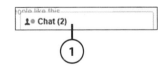

(1) Click the Chat gadget at the bottom-right corner of any Facebook page to display the full Chat panel.

(2) Click the name of the friend you want to chat with to open an individual Chat panel with the selected friend.

(3) If your friend has a webcam and is available to chat, you'll see a camera icon at the top of the Chat panel. Click this Start a Video Call button to initiate the video chat.

(4) When your friend answers the call, Facebook displays the video chat window. Your friend appears in the main part of the window; your picture is in a smaller window at the top left. All you have to do is talk.

(5) When you're ready to close the chat, mouse over the chat window and then click the X at the top-right corner.

Webcams and Microphones

Most webcams (whether attached or built in) also have built-in microphones. The camera in the webcam captures your picture, and the microphone in the webcam captures your voice. Just speak into the webcam to talk during a video chat.

>>>Go Further
VIDEO MESSAGES

If your friend is unavailable to chat, Facebook prompts you to leave a video message for that person. Your friend can then view and respond to that message when she's next online.

Click to like
this page

AARP's
Facebook Page

Status updates

In this chapter, you find out how to follow companies and public figures on Facebook.

→ Finding Companies and Public Figures on Facebook
→ Following Companies and Public Figures on Facebook
→ Managing the Pages You Follow

Liking Pages from Companies and Public Figures

Regular people on Facebook have their own Timeline pages. Businesses and public figures on Facebook, however, have their own special pages that are kind of like Timeline pages but different; they're tailored for the needs of customers and fans. These pages—rather unimaginatively called *Facebook Pages*—are how you keep abreast of what your favorite brands, products, and famous people are up to.

Finding Companies and Public Figures on Facebook

Even though businesses, celebrities, and public figures aren't regular users, they still want to use Facebook to connect with their customers and fans. They do this through Facebook pages—essentially Timeline pages for companies and public figures. If you're a fan of a given company or celebrity, you can "like" that entity's Facebook page—and keep abreast of what that company or individual is up to. It's kind of like joining an online fan club through Facebook.

Search for Companies and Public Figures

Many companies and organizations have Facebook pages for their brands and the products they sell. For example, you can find and follow pages for AARP, McDonalds, Starbucks, and Walmart on Facebook.

Many famous people—entertainers, athletes, news reporters, politicians, and the like—also have Facebook pages. So if you're a fan of Paul McCartney, Jack Nicklaus, Bill O'Reilly, or George Takei, you can follow any or all of them via the Facebook pages.

(1) Enter one or more keywords that describe the person, company, or organization into the Search box on the Facebook toolbar. As you type, Facebook displays a list of pages and people that match your query.

(2) If the page you want is listed, click it.

(3) If the page you want is not listed, click the Find All Pages Named entry to display a list of pages that match your query. Click the name of the page you want to view.

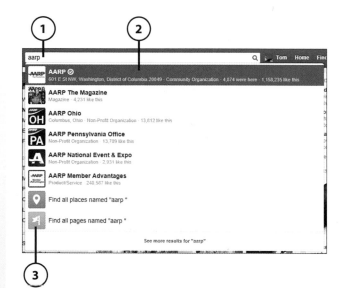

View a Facebook Page

A professional Facebook page is very similar to a personal Timeline page, right down to the timeline of updates and activities. Pages can feature specialized content, however, which is located at the top of the page, under the cover image. For example, a musician's page might feature an audio player for that performer's songs; other pages might let you view pictures and videos, or even purchase items online.

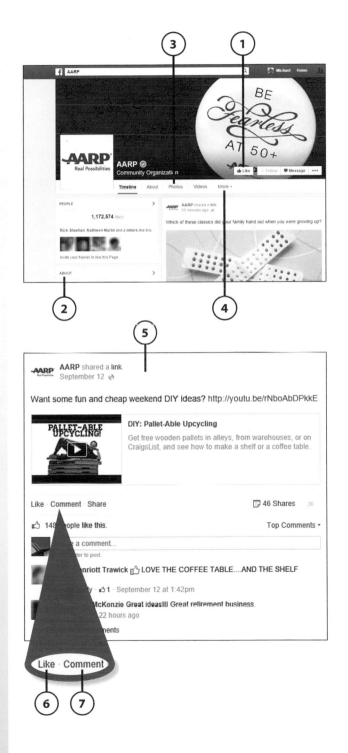

(1) Click the Like button to like (follow) this page.

(2) Click About to read more about this person or company.

(3) Click Photos to view the page's official pictures.

(4) Click any other content to view that content.

(5) Scroll down to view status updates and other postings.

(6) Click Like to like a specific post.

(7) Click Comment, and then type into the Comment box to leave a comment on a specific post.

>>>*Go Further*

WHO GETS OR HAS A PAGE?

Just about any public person or entity can create a Facebook page. You can create Facebook pages for businesses, brands, and products; for musicians, actors, and other celebrities; for politicians, public servants, and other public figures; and for school classes, public organizations, special events, and social causes.

If you want to create your own page for your business or community organization, go to www.facebook.com/pages/, click the Create Page button, and follow the onscreen instructions from there. To create a page you must be an official representative of the group or company behind the page; fans can't create official pages for the companies and entertainers they follow.

Following Companies and Public Figures on Facebook

Most companies and famous people on Facebook use their pages to keep their customers or fans informed of news and events. Some companies use their pages to offer promotions and special offers to customers.

Updates from a given company or celebrity appear on that entity's Facebook page. Some—but not all—posts from this entity also show up in your News Feed.

>>>*Go Further*

PROMOTED VERSUS ORGANIC POSTS

Facebook used to display all posts from those pages you like in your News Feed. It doesn't do that anymore. That's because Facebook is in the business of making money, and one way it does that is to charge companies to "promote" their page posts.

When a post is promoted (that is, paid for), Facebook displays it in the News Feeds of all of that page's followers. If a post is not promoted, Facebook probably won't display that post. If a company wants its followers to see its posts, it pretty much has to pay for that privilege.

Although some nonpromoted posts may show up in your News Feed from time to time, Facebook displays less than 20% of a page's "organic" (non-paid) posts. In other words, signing up to like a given page does not guarantee that you'll see all (or even most) of the posts to that page. If you want to see all that a company or person is posting, you have to go to that page to read the posts directly—or view your pages feed, which is covered later in this chapter.

Like a Facebook Page

A celebrity or company on Facebook can't be your friend; that is, you can't add a professional page to your Facebook friends list. Instead, you can choose to *like* that page so that you can follow all the posts made by that entity. Unlike friending an individual, the pages you like do not follow all the status updates that you make on a regular basis. You can begin following a page by using one of the following options.

Liking
Liking is a one-way thing. When you like a page you follow that page, but that page doesn't follow you.

1. From any list of pages, click the Like button to follow a specific page.

2. From a company or celebrity's Facebook page, click the Like button to follow that page.

View Posts in Your Pages Feed

Obviously, you can visit a given page to view the latest updates and content. You can also view updates from all the pages you like in Facebook's pages feed, which is kind of hidden in the navigation sidebar. The pages feed is kind of like a News Feed for the pages you've liked, not for the individuals you're friends with.

(1) On the Facebook toolbar, click Home to display your Home page.

(2) On your Home page, scroll down the navigation sidebar to the Pages section.

(3) Click Pages Feed to display the Pages feed in place of the normal News Feed.

(4) Posts from all the pages you follow are listed in the Pages feed, newest first. Scroll down to view more posts.

(5) Click Like to like a status update.

(6) Click Comment and type into the Comment box to comment on an update.

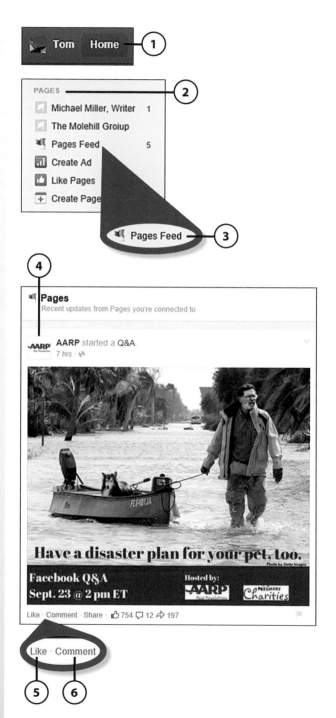

7 To return to the normal News Feed, click News Feed in the navigation sidebar.

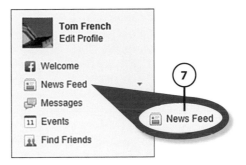

Managing the Pages You Follow

Some people only follow a handful of professional Facebook pages. Others find dozens of pages to follow. If you're a more prolific follower, you might want to manage your pages list over time.

View Your Favorite Pages

Not sure of whom exactly you're following? Then it's time to display all your favorite Facebook pages, in the pages list.

1 Click your name in the Facebook toolbar to display your Timeline page.

2 Click More under your cover image and select Likes to display those pages you've liked.

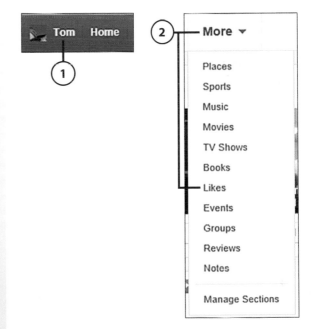

3 Click the type of page you're looking for—Interests, Foods, Activities, and so on.

4 Click any given image to display that specific page.

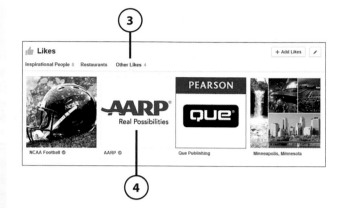

Unlike a Page

Just because you liked a given company or celebrity at one point in time doesn't mean you'll continue to like that entity forever. Your tastes change, after all, or you might find you don't like the posts a given page is making.

When you find yourself not liking a page so much, you can "unlike" that page. Unliking a page removes it from your Following feed, so you won't receive any more status updates or notifications from it.

1 From your Timeline page, click More, and then click Likes to display all the pages you currently like.

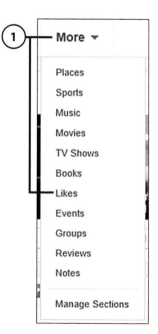

2 Mouse over the image for the page you no longer like and then mouse over the Liked button to display a menu of options.

3 Click Unlike.

Re-liking

You can always re-like an unliked page in the future. Just repeat the steps in the "Like a Facebook Page" section, earlier in this chapter, to like the page, and you'll be following it again.

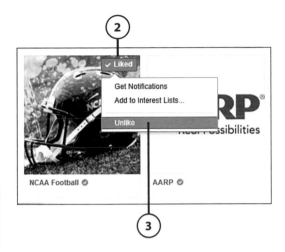

Group page   Post a message   View group
to the group   photos

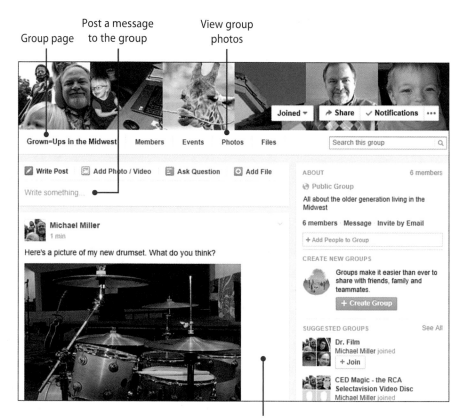

Group posts

In this chapter, you find out how to find and participate in interesting Facebook groups.

→ Finding and Joining Facebook Groups
→ Participating in Facebook Groups
→ Creating Your Own Facebook Group

13

Participating in Alumni and Nostalgia Groups

As you read in the previous chapter, Facebook Pages are like fan clubs for companies and celebrities and other public figures. There are other kinds of "clubs" on Facebook, however, in the form of public *groups*. Facebook has groups for all types of interests, from quilting to photography to golf.

Many of you are probably interested in groups that reunite you with people you've known in the past. These could be groups devoted to your old town or neighborhood, your old grade school or high school, or even activities you used to participate in. These groups are great ways to reminisce about the old times and keep in touch with people you knew back then.

Finding and Joining Facebook Groups

If you want to make new friends—and reconnect with old ones—one of the best ways to do so is to search out others who share your interests. If you're into gardening, look for gardeners. If you're into recreational vehicles, look for fellow RVers. If you're a wine lover, look for other connoisseurs of the grape.

Even better, look for people who've shared your life experiences. That means connecting with people who went to the same schools, lived in the same neighborhoods, and participated in the same activities.

You can find people who share your history and hobbies in Facebook *groups*. A group takes the form of a special Facebook page, a place for people interested in that topic to meet online and exchange information and pleasantries.

Search for Groups

Facebook offers tens of thousands of different groups online, so chances are you can find one or more that suit you. The key is finding a particular group that matches what you're interested in—which you do by searching.

(**1**) Go to the search box in the Facebook toolbar and enter one or more keywords that describe what you're looking for. For example, if you're interested in sewing, enter **sewing**. If you're looking for a group for graduates from your old high school, enter **high school name alumni**. (Replace *high school name* with the name of your high school, of course.) If you want to find a group created by people who live on the west side of Indianapolis, enter **Indianapolis west side**.

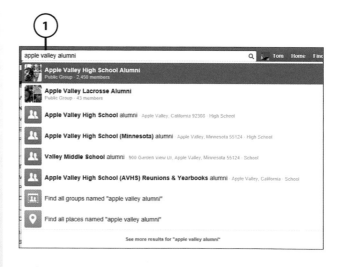

2 As you type, Facebook displays a list of items that match your query. If you see an interesting group in this list, click it.

3 If you don't see any matching groups in this short list, click the Find All Groups Named entry to display a page of groups that match your query.

4 For each group listed, you see a short description of the group and how many people are members. To view a group's Facebook page, click the name of the group.

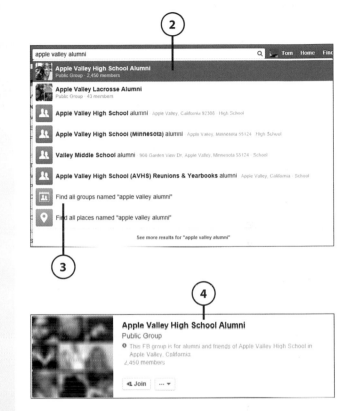

Browse for Groups

There are also several ways to browse for Facebook groups—by following Facebook's suggestions, exploring groups that your friends belong to, and viewing groups for your local area.

1 On Facebook's Home page, scroll down the navigation sidebar to the Groups section and click Find New Groups. This displays the Browse Groups page.

(2) By default, the Suggested Groups tab is selected. This page lists those groups in which Facebook thinks you might be interested.

(3) Click the Friends' Groups tab to view groups that your Facebook friends have joined.

(4) Click the Local Groups tab to view groups located in your area, such as those for local schools, organizations, and towns.

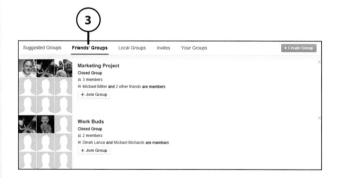

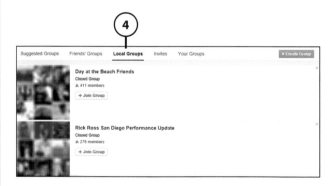

Join a Group

After you find a group, you can offi-
cially join it—and then participate
to whatever degree suits your fancy.
You can join a group from the search
results page, or from the group's
Facebook page.

Marketing Project
Closed Group
3 members
Michael Miller and 2 other friends are members
+ Join Group

1

1. To join a group from the Browse
   Groups page or any search
   results page, click the Join
   Group button.

Join this group to post and comment.   + Join Group

2

2. To join a group from its Facebook page, click Join Group.

> >>>*Go Further*
PUBLIC AND CLOSED GROUPS

Most groups are classified as Public groups, meaning they're open for all Facebook members to join. Some groups, however, are Closed groups, which require that the group
administrator approve all requests for membership.

To join a Closed group, you must apply for membership, and hope that your request is
granted. When you click the Join button, a request goes to the group administrator. If your
request is granted, you receive a message that you've been approved and are now an official member of the group. If your request is not granted, you don't get any response.

Participating in Facebook Groups

What can you do in a Facebook group? A lot, actually. You can read the latest news, discover new information, view photos and movies, exchange messages with other group members, and engage in online discussions about the
topic at hand. It's just like participating in a real-world club, except you do it all
on Facebook.

Visit a Group Page

Although you can view a feed of messages from all your groups (covered later in this chapter), most people prefer to visit individual group pages. This enables you to partake in all of the resources available in a given group.

GROUPS

Grown=Ups in the...

Wednesday Buds

Twin Cities Writers

Create Group

Manage Your Groups

Find New Groups

Manage Your Groups

(1) On Facebook's Home page, scroll down the navigation sidebar to the Groups section and click Manage Your Groups. This displays the Browse Groups page.

(2) Scroll down to the Groups You're In section and click the name of a group to open its Facebook page.

GROUPS YOU'RE IN

Old Time Indy's long missed businesses, and forgotten history. 20+   ✓ Added to Favorites ⚙

Ben Davis - Where is "and/or" Do you remember 20+   ✓ Added to Favorites ⚙

The Great Drummer's Group 20+   + Add to Favorites ⚙

Ludwig vintage snares and drums 20+   + Add to Favorites ⚙

Read and Reply to Messages

After you open a group page, you can read messages posted by other members of the group and then like and comment on those messages as you would normal Facebook status updates.

Group Posts

Posts that you make on a group's Facebook page are only displayed on that page, not in individual members' News Feeds.

1. Open the group's page and view all posts from members in the scrolling feed in the middle of the page.

2. Click Like to like a particular post.

3. Click Comment to reply to a post and then enter your reply into the Comment box.

4. Click Share to share a post with your Facebook friends in your Facebook feed.

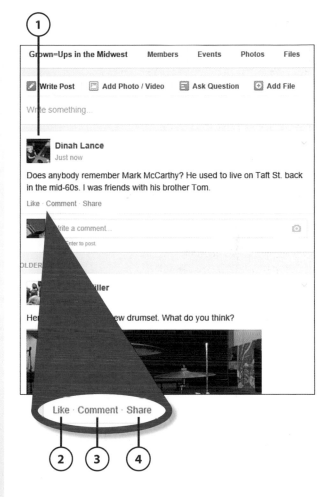

Post a New Message

Not only can you reply to posts made by other members, you can start a new discussion by posting a new message on the group's page. Other group members can then like and reply to your message.

(1) Open the group's page, scroll to the Publisher box, and click Write Post.

(2) Enter your message into the Write Something box; this expands the box.

(3) Click the Tag People in Your Post button to tag another friend in this post.

(4) Click the Add a Location to Post button to add a location to this post.

(5) Click the Choose a File to Upload (camera) button to add one or more photographs to this post.

(6) Click the Post button to post your message to the group.

View Group Members

Who belongs to this particular group? It's easy to view all the members of a Facebook group.

(1) Open the group's page and click Members to display a list of group members.

(2) To search for a particular member, enter that person's name into the Find a Member box and press Enter.

(3) Mouse over a member's name to view more information about that person.

(4) To add a group member as a friend, click Add Friend.

(5) To view a person's Timeline page, click that member's name.

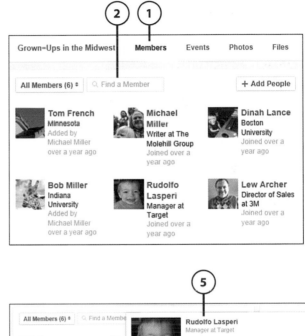

View Group Photos

Most groups let members post photos (and, in some cases, videos) of interest to other group members. If you're a member of a crafts group, for example, members might post photos of projects they've created. If you're a member of a group of old high school friends, members might post old photos from your school days. Viewing group photos, then, can be a fun activity.

1. Open the group's page and click Photos to display a list of group photos and photo albums.

2. Click a photo album to view all the photos in that album.

3. Click an individual photo to view that photo in a larger lightbox.

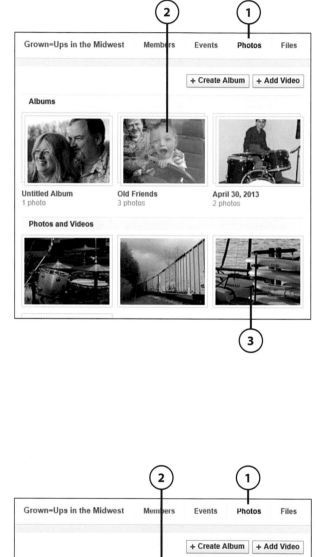

Upload Photos to the Group

You can upload your own photos to a group. This is a great way to share your activities with other group members.

1. Open the group's page and click Photos to display the group photos page.

2. Open the album to which you want to upload your photos.

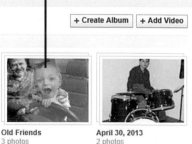

No Album

If your group doesn't yet have any photo albums, click the Upload Photos button on the main photos page. After you choose the photo(s) to upload, you're prompted to create a new photo album.

(3) Click Add Photos to display the Choose Files to Upload or Open dialog box.

(4) Select the photo or photos you want to upload.

(5) Click the Open button.

(6) Enter a short description of the photo into the Say Something About This Photo box.

(7) Click the Who Are You With? button to tag a person in this photo.

(8) Click the Where Are You? button to add a location to this photo.

(9) Click the Post Photos button to add these photos to the group.

Uploading Videos

You can also upload your own videos to a group. Go to the main photos page, click the Add Video button, and then proceed from there.

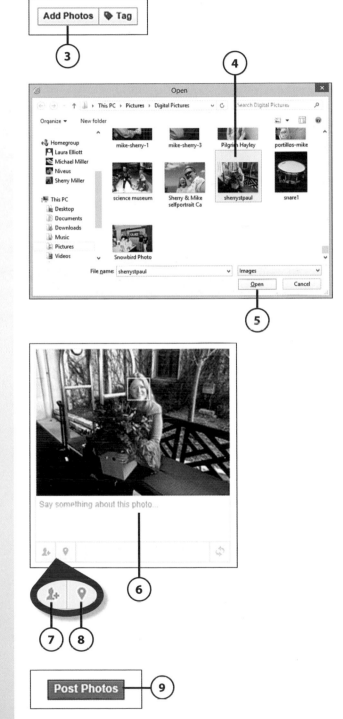

Get Notified of Group Activity

If you're active in a Facebook group, you might want to be notified when others post to the group. You can opt to receive notifications of each post made, or only of those posts made by your friends.

(**1**) Open the group's page and click Notifications.

(**2**) To receive a notification whenever a post is made to the group, select All Posts.

(**3**) To receive a notification whenever one of your Facebook friends posts to this group, select Friends' Posts.

(**4**) To not receive any notifications from this group, select Off.

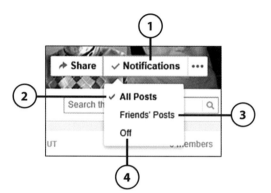

Leave a Group

If you grow tired of irrelevant or uninteresting posts in a given group, you can choose to unsubscribe from or leave a group.

(**1**) On Facebook's Home page, scroll down the navigation sidebar to the Groups section and click Manage Your Groups. This displays the Browse Groups page.

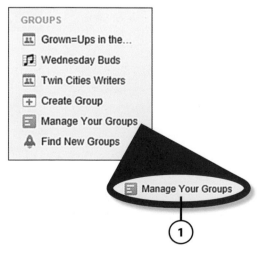

② Scroll down to the Groups You're In section, and find the group you want to leave.

③ Click the gear button for that group, and then click Leave Group.

④ Check the Prevent Other Members of This Group from Re-Adding You option.

⑤ Click the Leave Group button.

GROUPS YOU'RE IN

Old Time Indy's long missed businesses, and forgotten history. 20+   ✓ Added to Favorites

Ben Davis - Where is "and/or" Do you remember 20+   ✓ Added to Favorites

The Great Drummer's Group 20+   Edit Notification Settings
                                         Leave Group

Ludwig vintage snares and drums 20+   + Add to Favorites

Leave Ben Davis - Where is "and/or" Do you remember

Are you sure you want to leave this group?

☑ Prevent other members of this group from re-adding you.

Report Group   Leave Group   Cancel

>>>Go Further

USING GROUPS TO RECONNECT WITH OLD FRIENDS

On the surface, it's easy to think of Facebook groups as 21st-century versions of the home-room clubs you had back in high school. You know: chess club, knitting club, model airplane club, and the like.

Although there certainly are a huge number of these club-like Facebook groups, there are also groups that are more about times and places than they are about hobbies and interests. As such, these groups attempt to reconnect people with shared experiences.

I belong to a number of groups that connect me back to the days of my youth. For example, I grew up on the west side of Indianapolis, and now I belong to a Facebook group called Growing Up on Indy's Westside. It's a fun little group, with people posting faded pictures of old haunts, and lots of discussions about the way things used to be and what we used to do back then. I can't say I contribute too often, but it's always fun to read what others post.

I also belong to a "Where is and/or who do you remember?" group for my high school. This is a great place to find out what my old classmates have been up to in the decades since graduation, and it has lots of posts asking about individual students, teachers, and events. It's a nice stroll down memory lane.

The point is, participating in Facebook groups can be a great way to reconnect with your past. You might even meet up with some of your old friends in these groups, or make some new friends you should have made way back then. It's kind of a virtual blast from the past, and we have the Facebook social network to thank for it.

Creating Your Own Facebook Group

There are tens of thousands of groups already on Facebook, so chances are you can find one for whatever interests you. But if there isn't a group for your particular interest, you can create one—which is pretty easy to do.

Create a New Group

You can create a new group about any topic you like. You might want to create a group for a given hobby, event, or location. For example, if you're holding a class reunion, you could create a group to host posts and photos about the reunion.

(1) On Facebook's Home page, scroll down the navigation sidebar to the Groups section, and click Create Group. This displays the Create New Group panel.

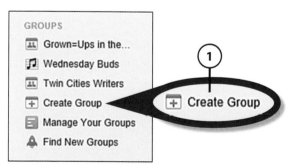

2 Enter the name of your new group into the Group Name box.

3 Enter the names of people you'd like to invite to your group into the Members box.

4 Choose whether you want the group to be Public (open to the general public), Closed to only those people whose member- ship requests you approve, or Secret to everyone except invited members.

5 Click the Create button.

6 Click the icon you want to repre- sent the group.

7 Click Okay to display the new group page.

8 To add a cover image to your group page, click either Upload Photo or Choose Photo, and select a picture.

9 To add a description of your group, click Add a Description.

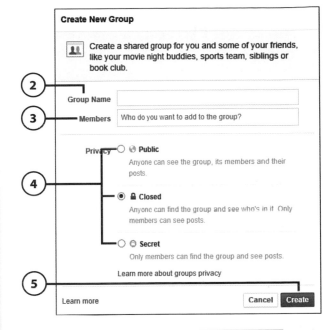

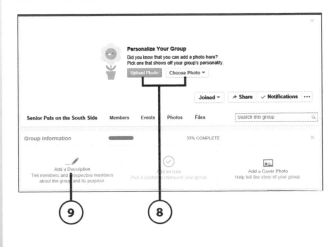

Invite Others to Join Your Group

After your new group is created, you might want to invite other people to join the group. (You can't rely just on people searching for your group to attract new members.) Chances are you have some Facebook friends who would probably like to participate; you can send them invitations to join.

1. Open your group's page and click the Members tab.

2. In the Members section, click the Add People button.

3. In the Add People to Group panel, enter the names of those Facebook friends you'd like to invite.

4. Click the Add button.

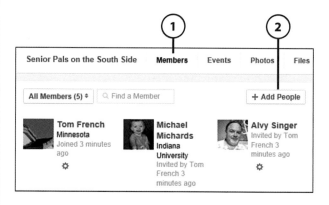

Send a Message to Group Members

As the administrator for your new group, you can send messages directly to all group members. This is a more direct means of communication than simply posting status updates to the group's Facebook page.

(**1**) On your group's page, go to the Publisher box and enter your message into the Write Something box.

(**2**) If you want to add a photo to this message, click Add Photo/Video and proceed from there.

(**3**) Click the Post button to post this message to members of the group.

Facebook event

Click to accept or decline
event invitation

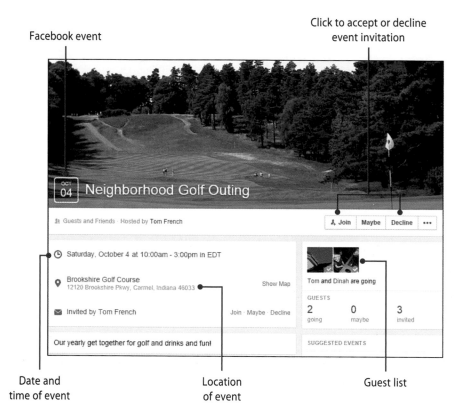

Date and
time of event

Location
of event

Guest list

In this chapter, you find out how to respond to event notifications and schedule your own events on Facebook—as well as celebrate your friends' birthdays online.

→ Dealing with Invitations to Events
→ Scheduling a New Event
→ Celebrating Birthdays

Attending Events and Celebrating Birthdays

Facebook lets you do more than just post and read status updates to and from your friends and family. You can also use Facebook as a kind of event scheduler, so you can manage parties, meetings, reunions, and the like from within Facebook.

The most common type of event is a birthday, and Facebook helps out there, too. Facebook notifies you of your friends' and family members' upcoming birthdays and makes it easy for you to send your birthday greetings. Facebook even announces your birthday to your friends—so sit back and wait for those well wishes to arrive!

Dealing with Invitations to Events

You use Facebook to keep in touch with all your friends and family, so it's only natural to use Facebook to schedule events that might involve these same people. You're all online and on Facebook, after all; why not use Facebook to notify people of upcoming events?

Facebook's events feature lets you do just that—schedule events and invite your Facebook friends to those events, using Facebook's built-in messaging system. In effect, Facebook creates a new page for each event scheduled, and whoever creates the event can then invite people to view the page and attend the event. If you receive an invitation to a Facebook event, you can then decide to accept or decline the invitation.

Respond to an Event Invitation in Your News Feed

When you've been invited to an event, a status update to that effect appears in your Facebook News Feed. You can respond to the event directly from that status update.

No Obligation
You should feel no obligation to accept any specific event. Only accept those you genuinely want to and can attend.

1. Go to your News Feed and scroll to the status update that contains the event invitation.

2. Click Join to accept the invitation. (In Facebook terminology, when you accept an invitation you "join" the event.)

3. Click the name of the event to display the event page.

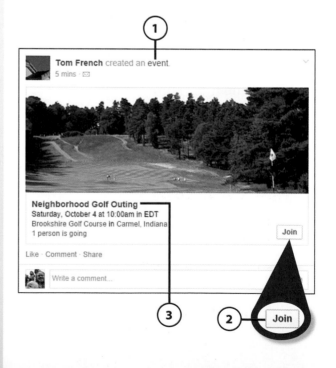

4 You can also respond to the event from the event page, if you haven't already joined the event. Click Join to accept the invitation.

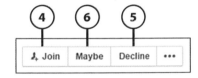

5 Click Decline if you don't want to accept the invitation.

6 Click Maybe if you're not sure whether or not you'll attend.

Respond to an Event Invitation in Your Notifications

Facebook also notifies you of upcoming events via its notification system. You can see all recent event invitations in the Notifications menu of the Facebook toolbar.

1 Click the Notifications button in the Facebook toolbar to see recent event invitations.

2 Click the event notification to display the event page.

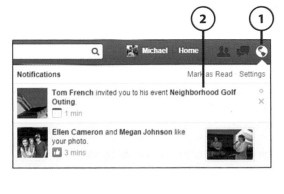

3 Click Join to accept the invitation.

4 Click Decline if you don't want to accept the invitation.

5 Click Maybe if you're not sure whether or not you'll attend.

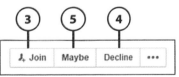

View an Event Page

When a friend schedules a new event, Facebook creates a page for that event. You can view the event page to learn more about the event.

(1) From your Facebook Home page, click Events in the navigation sidebar to display the Events page.

(2) To view all upcoming events, click Upcoming in the navigation sidebar. To view events on a calendar, click Calendar. To view past events, click Past.

(3) The Upcoming page displays all events to which you've been invited. Click the name of an event to view the page for that event.

(4) To accept the invitation to this event, click the Join button.

(5) To tell the host you won't be attending the event, click the Decline button.

(6) If you're not sure whether or not you're attending the event, click the Maybe button.

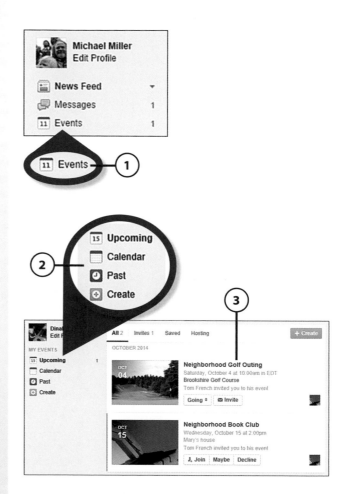

7 To see who's attending the event, click Going in the Guests box on the right.

8 To see who has been invited but hasn't yet responded, click Invited in the Guests box.

9 To view information about the event, see the date, time, and location beneath the cover image.

10 To view a map of the event's location, click Show Map.

11 View messages about this event in the feed beneath the information box.

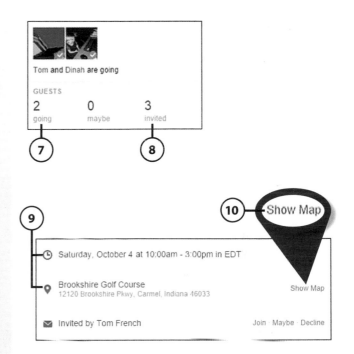

>>>*Go Further*

FACEBOOK EVENTS

What exactly is an event? On Facebook, an event is any item on your personal schedule. Events can be small and private, such as a doctor's appointment or dinner with a friend. Events can also be large and public, such as a community meeting or family reunion.

This means that you can use Facebook events to invite friends to backyard BBQs, block parties, golf dates, and card games. You can also use Facebook events to invite family members to birthday parties, holiday gatherings, and family reunions.

The events you create don't have to be real-world, physical events, either. You can schedule virtual events, such as inviting all your friends to watch a specific TV show or sporting event on a given evening. You can also schedule online events, such as seminars and conferences on sites that offer such options. In other words, you don't have to meet someone in person to share an event with them. It's all part of the social networking thing.

Scheduling a New Event

You don't have to wait to be invited to an event. You can also schedule your own Facebook events.

Maybe your neighborhood association has a meeting coming up. Maybe you're hosting a house party for some friends. Or maybe you just want to let everyone know about an upcoming anniversary. Whatever the case, Facebook makes it relatively easy to create new events and invite some or all of your Facebook friends to these events.

Create an Event

Facebook lets you create all manner of events, from parties to community meetings, and invite selected friends to those events. You can then manage that event through the event's Facebook page.

1. From Facebook's Home page, click Events in the navigation sidebar to display your Events page.

2. Click the Create Event button to display the Create New Event panel.

3. Enter the name of the event into the Name box.

4. Enter any additional details about the event into the Details box.

5. To specify the event's location, enter the location into the Where box.

Location

You can enter an exact address as the event's location, a city or state, or even just "My House" or "Room 223 in the Henry Building."

6. Enter the date of the event into the When section, or click the calendar icon and select a date from the calendar.

7. Enter the start time of the event into the Add a Time? box.

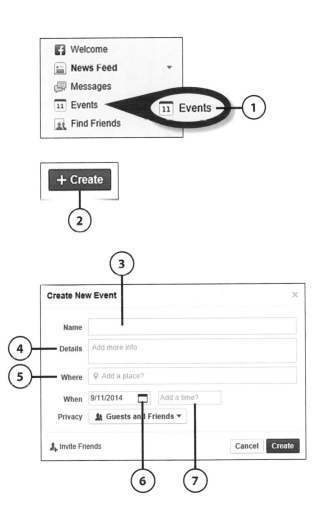

(8) If you entered a start time you can also enter an end time for the event. Click the End Time? link to display the End Time section, and then use the controls to set the end date and time.

(9) To invite friends to your event, click the Invite Friends link to display the Invite Friends panel.

(10) Check those friends you want to invite.

(11) Click the Save button to return to the Create New Event panel.

Create New Event ✕

Name	Neighborhood Book Club
Details	We're reading "The Help"
Where	⚲ Mary's house
When	10/15/2014 🗓	2:00 pm	CDT	End time? ——(8)
Privacy	👥 Guests and Friends ▾

👤 Invite Friends ———(9)   Cancel Create

——(10)

Invite Friends ✕

Search by Name ▾ | ✕

☐ 🖼 Lew Archer   ☐ 🖼 Michael Miller   ☐ 🖼 Michael Michards
☐ 🖼 Bob Miller   ☐ 🖼 Dinah Lance   ☐ 🖼 Alvy Singer

Guests can see who you invite. [?]   Save

——(11)

12 To determine who can see a given event, click the Privacy button and select Public, Open Invite, Guests and Friends, or Invite Only.

Public or Private

If you select Public, that event is visible to the general public. If you select Guests and Friends, it's visible to the people you invite and their friends. If you select Open Invite, it's visible to invited guests, their friends, and anyone else they happen to invite. If you select Invite Only, the event is visible only to the people you invite.

13 Click the Create button to create the event and send out the desired invitations.

Edit an Event

You can, at any time, edit the information for an event you've created. You can invite additional people, add or change details about the location and timing, and even post messages about the event.

1 From Facebook's Home page, click Events in the navigation sidebar to display your Events page.

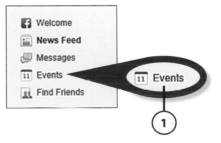

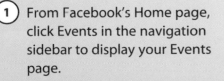

(2) Click the event you want to edit to display its Facebook page.

(3) Click the Add Event Photo to add a photo to accompany the event.

(4) Click the Invite button to invite additional friends to the event.

(5) Click the Edit button to display the Edit Event Info panel.

(6) Make the necessary changes to any of the information present.

(7) Click the Save button to return to the event page.

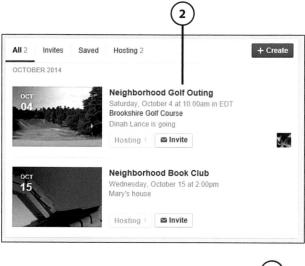

8 To post a message about the event, go to the Publisher box, click Write Post, enter your message, and then click the Post button.

| ✎ Write Post | 🖼 Add Photo / Video | ☰ Ask Question |

Write something…

👤₊ 📍 📷 😊   11 Neighborhood Book Club   **Post**

8

Cancel an Event

It happens. Even the best-laid plans go astray, and you may be forced to cancel a planned event. Here's how you do it.

| ✉ Invite | ✎ Edit | ••• |

1

1 Open the event page and click the Edit button to display the Edit Event Info panel.

2 Click Cancel Event.

3 Click the Yes button in the Cancel Event? dialog box.

Edit Event Info   ✕

Name	Neighborhood Book Club	✕
Details	We're reading "The Help"	
Where	📍 Mary's house	✕
When	10/15/2014 📅 2:00 pm CDT End time?
Hosts	Tom French
Privacy	👥 Guests and Friends ▾
	☑ Show guest list [?]

Cancel Event   Cancel   **Save**

2

Cancel Event?

Are you sure you want to cancel this event?

Yes No

3

Celebrating Birthdays

Facebook knows a lot about you and your friends, including when you were born. To that end, Facebook does a nice social service by letting you know when someone's birthday is approaching—so that you can send your birthday wishes.

Personal Replies

Most people receive a lot of Facebook greetings on their birthdays. Don't be disappointed if you don't receive a personal thank you from the birthday baby.

View Today's Birthdays

Facebook notifies you when it's one of your friends' birthday. You can then leave that person a happy birthday message. It's what people do on Facebook!

1. Click Home in the Facebook toolbar to display your Facebook Home page.

2. Today's birthdays are displayed in the notifications section near the top of the right-hand column. Click a birthday to display the Today's Birthdays panel.

3. Enter your message into the Write on Friend's Timeline box, and then press Enter.

Public Only

Facebook only notifies you of birthdays from friends who have opted to make their birthdates public. Friends with private birthdays do not appear in the birthday list.

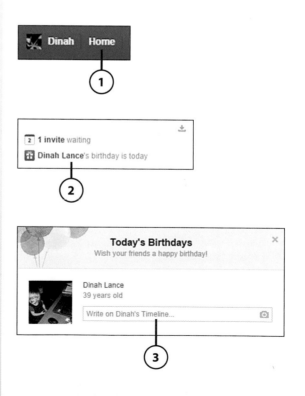

View Upcoming Birthdays

Facebook views a birthday as a kind of event and displays all upcoming birthdays on your Events page.

1. From the Facebook Home page, click Events in the navigation sidebar to display your Events page.

2. Click Calendar to view upcoming events in calendar view. Friends' birthdays appear as small thumbnail images on the calendar.

3. Mouse over a friend's thumbnail image to view that person's name and (in some cases) how old that person will be.

4. Click a friend's image to display that person's Timeline page.

5. Scroll to the Publisher box and click Post.

6. Enter your birthday greeting into the Write Something box.

7. Click the Post button to share your birthday greeting.

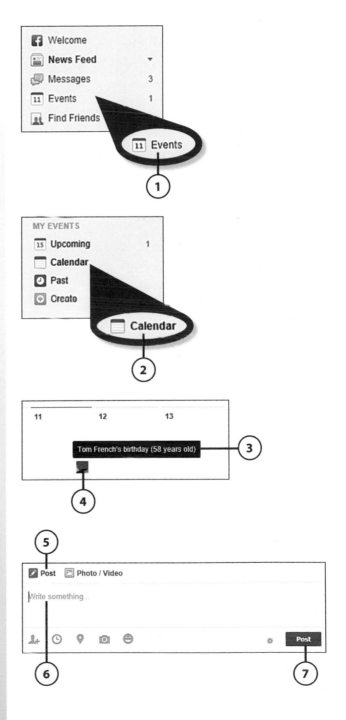

Explore Facebook's
Game Center.

Browse by
category.

Search for
specific games.

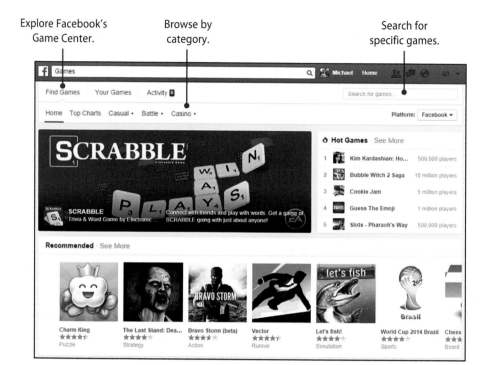

In this chapter, you find out how to have more fun on Facebook with social games.

→ Discovering Facebook Games
→ Playing Social Games on Facebook
→ Exploring Popular Apps and Games
→ Managing and Deleting Facebook Games

15

Playing Games

Millions of Facebook users of every age are going online to play games—either by themselves or with their Facebook friends. What kinds of games are available on Facebook? Read on to find out!

Discovering Facebook Games

Facebook offers a variety of fun and often addictive games for its users to play. These games, sometimes called *social games* (because you get to share scores and other game info with your friends), are played on the Facebook site itself, after you're logged in. Some of these are single-player games that you play yourself (versus the computer) or multi-player games that you play against your friends and other Facebook users. Some of these games have millions of players on Facebook!

You can find Facebook games in a variety of categories, including

- Action games
- Bingo games
- Board games
- Builder games
- Card games
- Casino games
- Match 3 games

- Puzzle games
- Role playing games
- Simulation games
- Sports games
- Strategy games
- Trivia games
- Word games

Third-Party Games

Most of the social games you find on Facebook are created by third-party application developers, not by Facebook itself. The vast majority of these games are available free of charge.

Browse for Games by Category

Facebook's Game Center is the place to go when you're looking for new apps and games. You can browse the Game Center by category to find what you're looking for.

(1) On Facebook's Home page, scroll down the navigation sidebar until you reach the Apps section, and then click Games.

2 This displays the Game Center page. Make sure the Find Games tab is selected.

3 The Home tab, underneath the Find Games tab, displays recommended and popular games in a variety of categories. Scroll down the page to view more games in more categories.

4 Click the Top Charts tab to view categories of the most popular games on Facebook, such as Most Popular, Popular Among Friends, and Top Grossing.

5 Click the Casual tab header to view games in the Puzzle, Board, Trivia & Word, Simulation, Match 3, Runner, Card, and Builders categories.

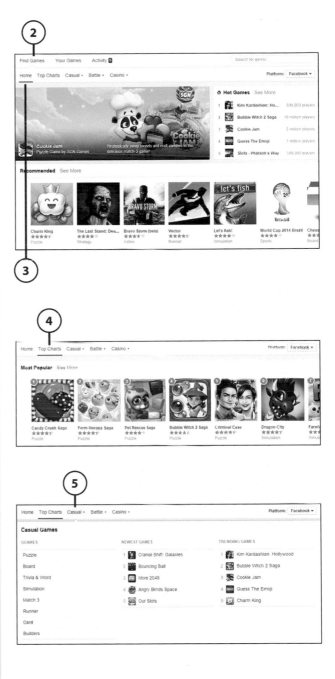

6 Click the Battle tab header to view games in the Action, Role Playing, Strategy, Card Battle, and Sports categories.

7 Click the Casino tab header to view games in the Slots, Poker & Table, and Bingo categories.

8 Click the name of a game to view that item's Facebook page—and start playing that game.

6

| Home | Top Charts | Casual ▾ | Battle ▾ | Casino ▾ | | | Platform: | Facebook ▾ |

Battle Games

GENRES		NEWEST GAMES		TRENDING GAMES	
Action	1	Snake	1	Monster Legends
Role Playing	2	No Limits	2	Bowling King
Strategy	3	Sword Quest	3	Marvel Avengers Alliance Tactics
Card Battle	4	BATTLE CRY (War RPG) - LIVE	4	Dino Hunter: Deadly Shores
Sports	5	Fairy Tail Online	5	Sports Heads Football 2

7

| Home | Top Charts | Casual ▾ | Battle ▾ | Casino ▾ | | | Platform: | Facebook ▾ |

Casino Games

GENRES	NEWEST GAMES	TRENDING GAMES	
Slots		1	Slots - Pharaoh's Way
Poker & Table		2	Gold Fish Casino Slots
Bingo		3	Bingo World
		4	Bingo USA
		5	Duck Dynasty Slots

Search for Specific Apps and Games

Browsing is a good way to see what games are available. But if you have a specific game in mind, you can search for it directly, which is quicker.

1 On Facebook's Home page, scroll down the navigation sidebar until you reach the Apps section, and then click Games to display the Game Center.

1 Games

APPS

Games
Pokes
Photos
Music
SCRABBLE
Bejeweled Blitz
Games Feed

(2) Enter the name of the game into the search box at the top-right corner of the page.

(3) As you type, Facebook displays those games that match your query. Click the name of an item to display its Facebook page.

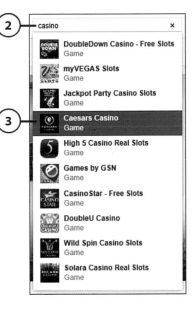

Playing Social Games on Facebook

Playing a game on Facebook is pretty much like playing any other game on your computer or mobile device. Here's how to start playing a game:

(1) From the Game Center, click the name of the game to open its Facebook page.

② Click the Play Now button to begin playing the game.

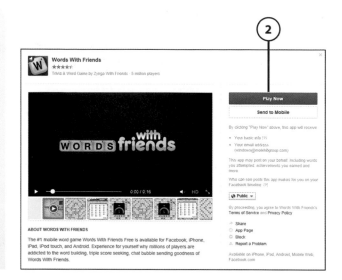

It's Not All Good

Social Games and Privacy

Many Facebook games are social in nature, in that they use your Facebook friends list to either obtain information about your friends or send information to them regarding your activity within the game. That's both good and bad.

One of the good things about a social game is that it helps to create a larger community of users by linking you with your friends. The game might also use your friends' information to provide additional benefit to you. (For example, a game might request that your friends send you in-game items or points.)

The bad thing about a social game is that it makes a lot of personal information public. When you agree to share your information (including your friends list) with the game, you're relinquishing some degree of privacy. You're also betraying the trust of your friends by letting the game access some of their personal information, or post annoying information to their News Feeds. You might be comfortable doing that, and that's fine. But some users don't want to make everything public, and especially don't want to breach their friends' privacy. If that's how you think, then don't sign up for social games that request you share this information. If you don't join in, you won't be jeopardizing your privacy.

Exploring Popular Apps and Games

Younger users certainly like to play games online, and so do older ones. Social games are a great way to fill those spare hours when you could be doing something more useful.

What types of games are most popular with more mature users? Here's a short list:

- **Bejeweled Blitz**—A single-player puzzle game.
- **Bingo Blitz**—An online bingo game that you can play with your friends and other Facebook users.
- **Brandomania**—A trivia game focusing on well-known (and lesser-known) brands and logos.
- **Caesar's Casino**—One of the most popular collections of casino games.
- **Candy Crush Saga**—The current number-one game on Facebook, a matching puzzle game.
- **Farm Heroes Saga**—A Candy Crush-like matching puzzle game.
- **Mahjong Trails**—The age-old game of Mahjong, on Facebook.
- **myVEGAS Slots**—Online slot machines.
- **Pepper Panic Saga**—From the makers of Candy Crush Saga, a similar matching puzzle game.
- **Pet Rescue Saga**—A Tetris-like puzzle game.
- **Scrabble**—The classic word game, online in Facebook.
- **Scramble with Friends**—A challenging word-finding game.
- **Solitaire Arena**—The classic single-player card game.
- **SongPop**—A pop music trivia game, for music lovers of all ages.
- **Texas HoldEm Poker**—Online poker with your Facebook friends.
- **Words with Friends**—A crossword-style word game you play with your Facebook friends.
- **World Poker Club**—Another popular online poker game.

Managing and Deleting Facebook Games

Over time you may find that you're playing certain games less and less—if at all. You can manage all the games you're playing from Facebook's Game Center, and delete those you no longer play.

1. On Facebook's Home page, scroll down the navigation sidebar until you reach the Apps section, and click Games to display the Game Center.

2. Click the Your Games tab to view those games you've installed.

3. Click the gear button for the game you want to manage or delete; this displays a management panel for that game.

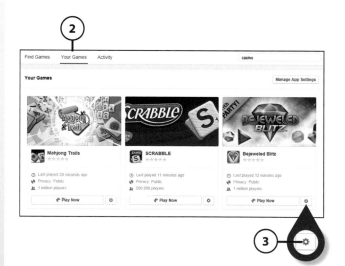

(4) To change who can see that you're playing this game, click the App Visibility button and select from these options: Public, Friends, Friends of Friends, Only Me, or Custom.

(5) To select whether or not the game can send you notifications, click the Send You Notifications button and select either Yes or No.

(6) To delete the game, click the Remove App link at the bottom of the panel.

(7) When prompted to confirm the removal, click the Remove button.

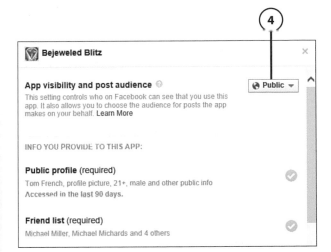

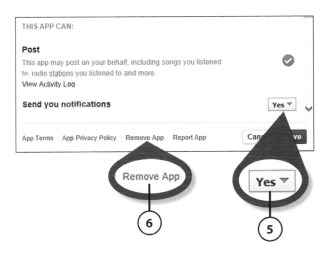

Search query

Map of matching businesses

Search results

Fine-tune your search

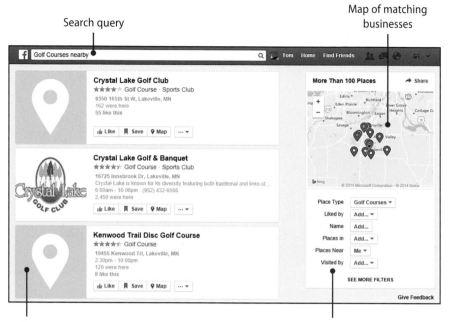

In this chapter, you find out how to search Facebook for people, places, and things.

Searching Facebook for Useful Information

If you think about it, Facebook knows an awful lot about you—mainly based on the personal information you've entered. Facebook knows where you live, where you have worked, where you went to school, and what you like. In addition, Facebook knows who your friends are, and it knows all those things about them, too.

It makes sense, then, to use Facebook as a search engine for useful and interesting information, much as you'd use Google or Yahoo! Yes, you can search Facebook for basic stuff, such as specific pages or groups or apps. But you can also search Facebook for more interesting connections, such as your friends who like a particular type of cuisine, or people in your hometown who watch a given TV show. Facebook is able to use what it knows about you and other users to create a huge database of information from which it can answer the most complicated search queries.

Understanding Facebook's Graph Search

There are more than one billion users of Facebook, and they all have their own histories, likes, and dislikes—all documented on the Facebook site. Facebook's Graph Search takes this collective information and uses it to answer both basic and complex questions posed by you and other users.

Most web search engines, such as Google, require you to enter one or more keywords to conduct a search. Graph Search, in contrast, is a natural language search engine that lets you enter plain English questions. All you have to do is ask a question, as you would in real life, and Graph Search provides the answers.

Those answers come from Facebook connecting what it knows about its one billion users, and the relationships between them. In Facebook parlance, the "graph" is this database of user information, and when you search Facebook, you're searching the graph—hence the term Graph Search.

Facebook focuses Graph Search on the likes and interests you enter in your personal profile. When you like a particular page or say you're interested in a given TV show, Facebook uses those pieces of information to answer somebody's future query.

For example, Facebook might know that you've listed gardening as an interest in your personal profile and that you live in North Carolina. If someone searches for gardening buffs in North Carolina, Facebook could identify you. Likewise, if you've liked the Starbucks Facebook page and one of your friends searches for the best coffee in North Carolina, Facebook can put two and two together and use your recommendation to tell your friend about Starbucks.

By connecting these facts with your likes and interests, it's easy enough to discover friends who've read books by a given author, or find out your friends' favorite restaurants in your hometown.

This means you can use Graph Search to search for all kinds of things. The following are some examples of natural ways you can search on Facebook:

- Friends who like NCIS and CSI
- Friends who've read books by Hemingway
- Restaurants in San Diego

- Hotels in Orlando my friends like
- Photos of golf courses in Phoenix
- People in Des Moines who listen to Tony Bennett

The answers you receive will be both personal and pertinent.

Using Facebook's Graph Search

You use Graph Search via the search box in the Facebook toolbar at the top of every Facebook page. The results that Facebook returns differ depending on what you search for, however.

Perform a Basic Search

To conduct a search, you must enter one or more words that describe what you're looking for. The more words you enter, the more refined the results will be. And remember, Graph Search is a natural language search, which means you can enter complete sentences. Instead of searching for **pizza**, search for **pizza in Chicago**; instead of searching for **class photos**, search for **photos of my college classmates**.

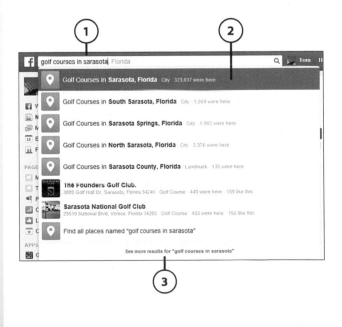

1. Click within the search box in the Facebook toolbar and begin typing your query. As you type, a list of suggestions appears beneath the search box.

2. If one of the suggestions matches what you're searching for, click it.

3. Alternatively, click More Results at the bottom of the list to display more search options.

(4) Click the item that best matches
what you're searching for.

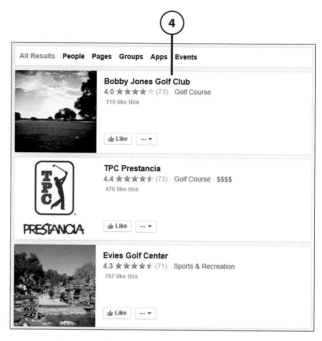

Understand Your Search Results

The search suggestions that Graph Search displays when you start typing in
the search box are just that—suggestions. If you search for **favorite musicians**, for example, you see suggestions for My Favorite Musicians, Musicians,
Favorite Musicians of My friends, and Groups, Pages, and Places named "favorite
musicians." If you search for **restaurants in Phoenix**, you see suggestions for different types of restaurants in that city.

**Suggested
searches for
"favorite
musicians"**

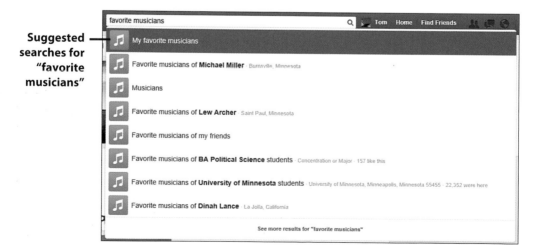

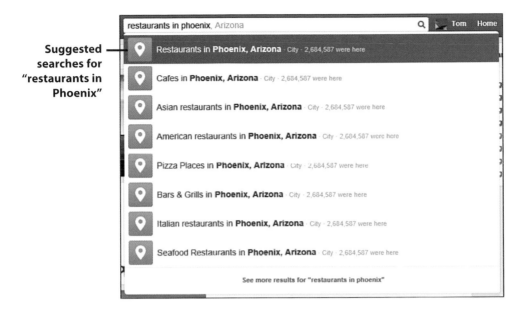

Suggested searches for "restaurants in Phoenix"

What you see when you click one of these suggestions differs by the type of suggestion. For example, clicking the restaurants in Phoenix suggestion displays a page of Phoenix restaurants popular among Facebook users, all displayed on a map of Phoenix. Click a restaurant's name to go to its Facebook page, or click the Any Cuisine button to filter the list by type of food served.

Click to select cuisine

Name of restaurant—click to view Facebook page

Click to view restaurant at this location

The results are much different for other suggestions, however. If you click one of the results of the **favorite musicians** search, such as **favorite musicians of my friends**, you see a list of performers liked by your Facebook friends. Click a name to view that performer's page, or click the Like button to like the group.

Paula Lammers Nightingale Jazz
Musician/Band
David Martin and other friends like this
176 like this
Sherry 'French Elliott' Miller, Sandi Simmons Cary and 4 other friends...

👍 Like   ··· ▼

— **Click to like musician**

David Martin/Mike Doolin — **Name of musician— click to view Facebook page**
Musician/Band
Laurel Costain Kaeferlein and other friends like this
276 like this
Megan Johnson, Sherry 'French Elliott' Miller and 3 other friends like t...

✓ Liked ▼   ··· ▼

Other searches display more direct results. Let's say you searched for **photos of my friends in Minnesota**. Click this search suggestion and you see exactly what you searched for—photos of your friends that were taken in Minnesota. Click on any photo to view it larger in its own lightbox.

Fine-Tune Your Search Results

Many search results pages let you fine-tune the results. Look for a search filter box on the right side of the search results page that lets you do just that; the options available differ depending on what you're searching for.

Options

As an example, if you search for **friends in California**, you find options for Gender, Relationship (for example, Single or Divorced), Employer, Current City, Hometown, School, and Friendship (My Friends, Friends of My Friends, and so forth).

---

(1) Enter your query into the search box and click a search suggestion to display the search results page.

(2) In the search filter box, click the button for the option you want to fine-tune, and then make a selection from the resulting list. The search results are updated accordingly.

My friends who live in **Los Angeles, California**

(1)

2 Friends   → Share

Gender	Add... ▼
Relationship	Add... ▼
Employer	Add... ▼
Current City	Los Angeles, California ▼
Hometown	Add... ▼
School	Add... ▼
Friendship	My Friends ▼ Add
Name	Add...

SEE MORE FILTERS

(2)

Searching for Specific Things

Now you know how Graph Search works, and how to use it, in general terms. Let's take specific looks at some of the more popular types of searches you can make with Graph Search.

Search for Facebook Pages or Groups

Although you can use Graph Search for very sophisticated and personal searches, you can also use it to search for company or celebrity pages on the Facebook site, as well as interest-oriented Facebook groups.

(1) Click within the search box in the Facebook toolbar and begin typing the name of the entity or topic. As you type, a list of suggestions appears beneath the search box.

(2) It's likely that the page or group you're looking for will appear near the top of the search suggestions. If so, click it to go to that page or group.

(3) Alternatively, click the Find All Pages Named or Find All People Named option to view a list of suggested pages, and then click the item you want.

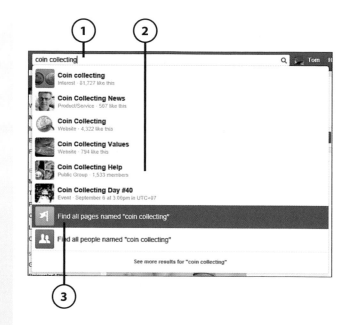

Search for Games and Apps

You can also use Graph Search to search for apps and games you might want to use and play.

(1) Click within the search box in the Facebook toolbar and begin typing the name of the app or game.

(2) It's likely that one of the suggestions will be the app or game you're looking for. If so, click that item to go to the item's Facebook page.

(3) Alternatively, click Find All Apps Named to display additional games or apps, and then click the one you want.

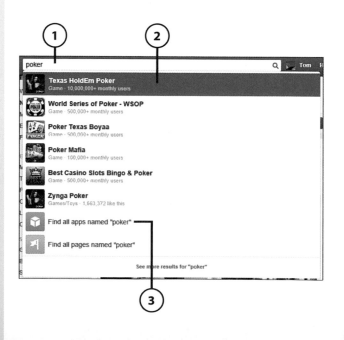

Search for People

One of the more popular uses of Graph Search is to look for specific friends on Facebook. Chapter 2, "Finding Old (and New) Friends on Facebook," covers how to search for old friends, but Graph Search gives you even more options for tracking down long-lost friends—particularly in establishing connections between other friends you already know of.

(1) To search for a person by name only, enter that person's name, like this: **people named john doe**.

(2) To search for a person by name and current location, enter the person's name and location, like this: **people named john doe in Minneapolis**.

(3) To search for a person by where they grew up, enter the person's name and hometown, like this: **people named john doe who lived in Kokomo**.

(4) To search for a person by where they went to school, enter the person's name and school, like this: **people named john doe who went to school at Indiana University.**

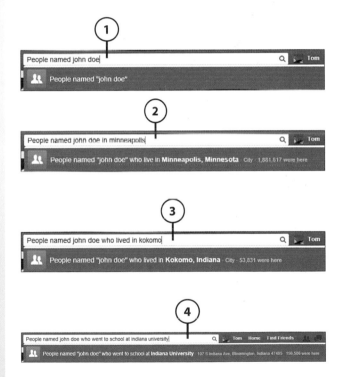

5 To search for a person by where they used to work, enter the person's name and company, like this: **people named john doe who worked at General Mills**.

6 Sometimes the best approach is to search through friends of your friends. To search for a person in your friends' friends lists, enter the person's name like this: **people named john doe who are friends of my friends**.

7 Or, you can just search through all the friends of a specific friend, like this: **friends of dinah lance**.

8 To search for friends of your friends who currently live near you (or any specific location), enter the location like this: **friends of my friends who live near Raleigh**.

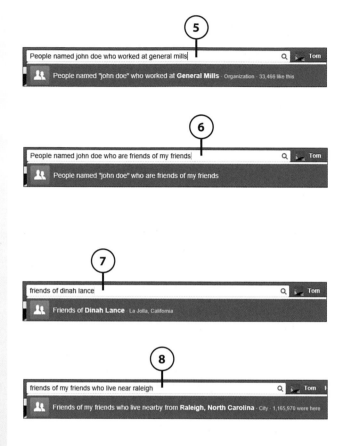

5

People named john doe who worked at general mills

People named "john doe" who worked at **General Mills** · Organization · 33,466 like this

6

People named john doe who are friends of my friends

People named "john doe" who are friends of my friends

7

friends of dinah lance

Friends of **Dinah Lance** · La Jolla, California

8

friends of my friends who live near raleigh

Friends of my friends who live nearby from **Raleigh, North Carolina** · City · 1,165,970 were here

Search for Local Businesses

Are you looking for a good Italian restaurant to have dinner at? Or maybe a decent local hardware store? What about a hotel to stay at on an upcoming vacation? Facebook's Graph Search can help you find all these businesses, and more.

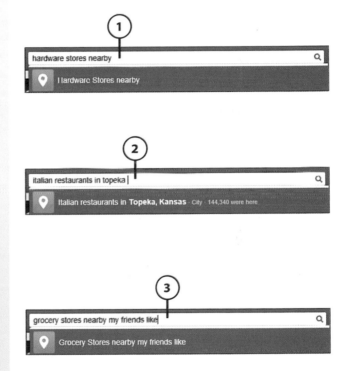

1. To search for a type of business near your current location, enter this: *business* **nearby**. For example, to search for a nearby hardware store, enter: **hardware stores nearby**.

2. To search for a business in another location, enter the location and type of business, like this: *business* **in location**. For example, to look for an Italian restaurant in Topeka, enter: **Italian restaurants in Topeka**.

3. To narrow your search to businesses that your friends like, add **my friends like** to your query. For example, to look for nearby grocery stores that your friends like, enter **grocery stores nearby my friends like**.

Search for Books, Movies, and Music

Graph Search can be a good way to find other things you might like. For example, if a lot of your friends like a particular book, you might like it, too. The nice thing about this type of search is that Facebook shows you which of your friends liked a particular item; you can then base your decision on who liked what.

① To search for books you might like, enter **favorite books of my friends**.

② To search for movies you might like, enter **favorite movies of my friends**.

③ To search for TV shows you might like, enter **favorite TV shows of my friends**.

①

favorite books of my friends

Favorite books of my friends

②

favorite movies of my friends

Favorite movies of my friends

③

favorite tv shows of my friends

Favorite TV shows of my friends

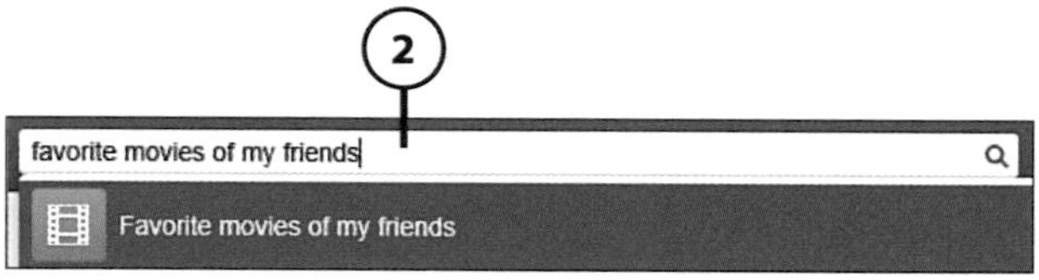

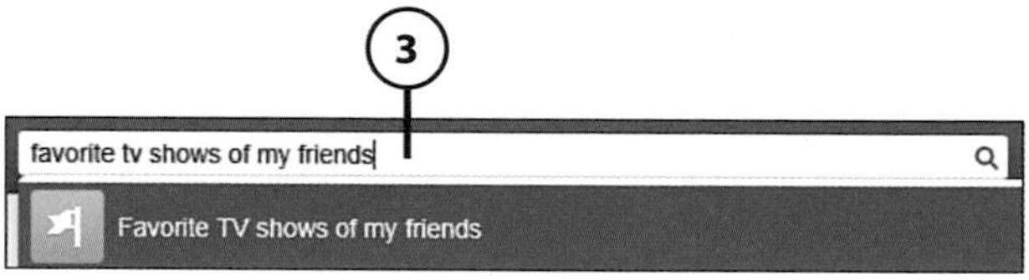

Search for Photos

Facebook is the largest photo-sharing site in the world, but it can be tough to find those specific pictures you're looking for. That's where Graph Search comes in. Just enter a detailed description of what you're looking for, and Graph Search finds the best photos that match your query.

1 To search for photos of a particular location or landmark, enter **photos of location**. For example, to see photos of the Statue of Liberty, enter **photos of Statue of Liberty**.

2 To search for photos taken in a particular city or state, enter **photos taken in location**. For example, to see pictures taken in Orlando, enter **photos taken in Orlando**.

3 To view photos of a particular item or object, enter **photos of object**. For example, to view photos of parrots, enter **photos of parrots**.

4 To view photos of a particular location or object taken by your friends, add **uploaded by my friends** to your query. For example, to search for photos your friends have taken in La Jolla Cove, enter **photos of La Jolla Cove uploaded by my friends**.

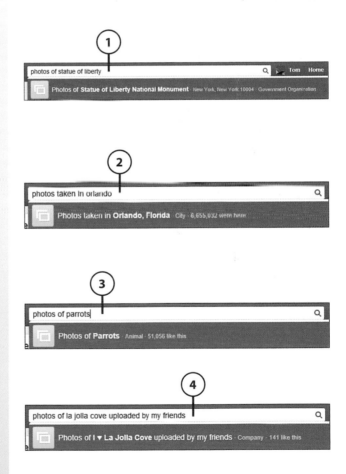

Picture posted by grandkids
(by their parent)

Dinah Lance
Just now ·

We miss you, Grandpa!

Like · Comment · Share

Write a comment...

Press Enter to post.

In this chapter, you discover the best ways to use Facebook to get closer to the youngest members of your family.

→ Are Kids Still Using Facebook?
→ How to Connect with Younger Users on Facebook
→ Five Things *Not* to Do with Your Grandkids on Facebook
→ Other Places You'll Find Your Kids and Grandkids Online

17

Keeping in Touch with Your Kids and Grandkids on Facebook

Facebook is very popular among middle-aged and older users today, but it started out as a social network for college students. While the current generation of college students has moved onto newer, hipper social media for their own personal use, most younger users still maintain a presence on Facebook—primarily to keep in touch with the older members of their families.

Are Kids Still Using Facebook?

Facebook might be new to you, but it's old news for most younger users. In fact, Facebook used to be the place where all the cool kids hung out. That was probably before you signed up, however. Today, Facebook's user base has shifted toward the older side, and younger users are either using Facebook less or abandoning it completely.

Let's face it—if you're a kid, you don't want to do much of anything that your parents and grandparents are also doing. A website or social network just isn't cool if all the older people you know are using it, too.

And older users definitely are using Facebook. The fastest growing age group on Facebook today is users aged 55 and up, whereas users 35 and up now represent almost half of Facebook's user base. This means that kids in their teens and twenties make up less than half of all Facebook users—even though they used to rule the roost.

This demographic shift is due in part to more older people joining up, but also to equally large numbers of younger users leaving. From 2011 to 2014, Facebook lost more than 3 million users aged 13 to 17, and another 3 million in the 18 to 24 age group. Like it or not, Facebook is definitely becoming a hangout for older users.

Before this shift, Facebook used to be a good place for parents and grandparents to connect with their kids and grandkids. That's less true today, although there's still a place for Facebook in the intergenerational communication chain.

Even though a lot of younger users are leaving Facebook for good, even more are remaining on Facebook but just using it less. Instead of checking in constantly throughout the day, today's younger generation of Facebook users are more likely to check in just once a day, or maybe once every few days.

In other words, your grandkids and their friends are maintaining their ties to the Facebook community, even as they explore new social networking opportunities elsewhere. Why stay on Facebook if it's no longer cool? To stay in touch with those non-cool older family members.

That's right—younger users recognize Facebook's valuable role in connecting all family members—younger and older. Your kids, grandkids, and nephews and nieces are staying on Facebook *because* you're there—not in spite of it. They know that you use Facebook to share family news and photos, and there's value in that. It's easier for them to keep up with what's going on by checking in on Facebook every few days. The younger generation might not be using Facebook to talk to one another as much anymore, but they're using it to talk to you and other people that are important to them.

Knowing this changes the way you might have otherwise used Facebook to connect with your grandkids. You no longer have to sneak around the dark corners of Facebook to keep tabs on what the kids are doing; instead, they expect you to be right up front with your comments and pictures and such.

How to Connect with Younger Users on Facebook

If you're in your sixties, your thirty-something and forty-something children are likely long-time Facebook users. They know how to use Facebook to share and connect with friends and family, and expect you to either do the same or learn how. You'll find them checking their Facebook feeds several times a day.

Your teenage and twenty-something children and grandchildren are also expert in using Facebook, but they use it a whole lot less. They check their News Feeds no more than a few times each week, primarily to see what their parents and other family members are up to. Some still use Facebook to keep in touch with distant friends, although this is becoming less common. Like their parents, these kids are savvy Facebook users, even if they're not on all the time.

Knowing this, you need to connect with your children and grandchildren at a similar level of expertise. You need to know not only how to connect via Facebook, but also what is best to share in that environment. Let's walk through what you need to do.

Make Friends with Your Kids and Grandkids

The first step in using Facebook to connect with your younger family members is to add them to your friends list. It shouldn't be too hard to find your children, grandchildren, nieces, and nephews on Facebook, and then send out the necessary friend requests. When your family members are on your friends list, every post they make should show up in your News Feed.

It's Not All Good

Selected Posts

By default, your kids' and grandkids' posts are visible to all their Facebook friends, including you. More tech-savvy youngsters, however, might figure out how to fine-tune their privacy settings and exclude you (and other family members) from some or all of their posts. This means you *don't* see everything they post in your News Feed. There's no way around this.

(1) Facebook might suggest your family members as friends when you first sign up or when you click the Friend Requests button on the toolbar—especially if you have their addresses in your email contacts list. If so, click the Add Friend button.

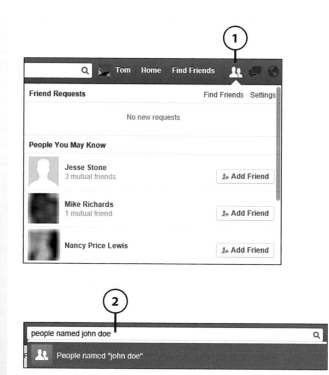

Finding Friends

Learn how to find family and friends on Facebook in Chapter 2, "Finding Old (and New) Friends on Facebook."

(2) Alternatively, you can do a simple search for your kids and grandkids on the Facebook site. Use the search box in the Facebook toolbar to search for **people named *john doe*** and your family member's name should pop up. (In this and other examples, replace "john doe" with the name of the person you're searching for.)

Put Your Family Members in a Special Friends List

Just as you can read your kids' and grandkids' posts on Facebook, they can also read your status updates in their News Feeds. However, your grandkids might not be interested in everything you post, especially those posts that deal with issues of interest to you and your friends.

The solution is to not send all your posts to the youngsters. Instead, you can create a *friends list* that contains only selected family members. You can then opt to hide your posts from members of that list—or send selected posts only to your family members. It's an easy way to deal with groups of people (in this instance, your family members) with a single click.

It's Not All Good

They Love You, But...

Depending on what you post on Facebook, your kids and grandkids might find your status updates charming. Or they might find them embarrassing or even totally uninteresting. Let's face it: The kinds of things that interest someone our age aren't likely to be engrossing to the average teenager. Sure, you played a good round of golf today, or got a good deal at the local discount store, but do your kids and grandkids really care about that? For that matter, all those words of wisdom and inspiration that you like to post are likely to be roundly ignored by youngsters with more immediate things on their minds.

In other words, don't expect the younger generations to like and comment on everything you post. At best, they might read your posts and then move on. At worst, they might figure out how to block your posts—or even unfriend you.

(1) Start by creating a new Facebook friends list that contains all your children and grandchildren. Go to the Timeline page for your first family member, click the Friends button, and then click Add to Another List.

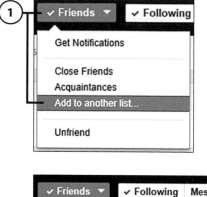

(2) Facebook creates a number of "smart" lists, based on personal information you've added to your account. One of these smart lists, named Family, is just for your family members. Click Family to add this person to your Family list.

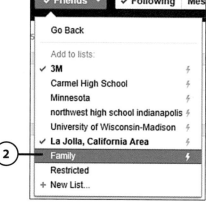

(3) For each of your other family members, go to his or her Timeline page, click the Friends button, and add him or her to your Family list.

4 Now you can configure your privacy settings so that your family members don't see the bulk of your posts. Click Privacy Shortcuts on the Facebook toolbar, select Who Can See My Stuff?, and then go to the Who Can See My Future Posts? section.

5 Click the privacy button, click More Options, and then select Custom to display the Custom Privacy pane.

6 Go to the Don't Share This With section and enter Family into the These People or Lists box.

7 Click the Save Changes button.

8 By default, all new posts you make are sent to all of your friends *except* the family members in your new friends list. To send a post to your family members only, click the privacy button within the post and select Custom to open the Custom Privacy pane.

9 In the Share This With box, click the X to remove the Friends item.

10 In the Don't Share This With box, click the X to remove the Family item.

11 In the Share This With box, type Family to enter the Family list.

12 Click Save Changes to return to your status update, and then click the Post button to send this update to all the members of your Family list.

Custom Privacy

Learn about Facebook's privacy settings in Chapter 18, "Managing Your Privacy on Facebook."

8

⚙ Custom ▾

Who should see this?

🌐 **Public**
Anyone on or off Facebook

👥 **Friends**
Your friends on Facebook

🔒 Only Me

✓ ⚙ Custom

📍 La Jolla, California Area

9   **11**

Custom Privacy   ✕

➕   **Share this with**

These people or lists   Friends ✕

Friends of tagged   ✔

Note: Anyone tagged can also see this post.

✕   **Don't share this with**

These people or lists   Family ✕ |

Facebook never reveals when you choose not to share a post with somebody.

Cancel   **Save Changes**

10   **12**

Send a Private Message

Facebook status updates are public, but sometimes you want to send a more personal message to your kids or grandkids. That's where Facebook's private messaging system comes in. You can easily send a private message to your favorite family member, and no one else will see it.

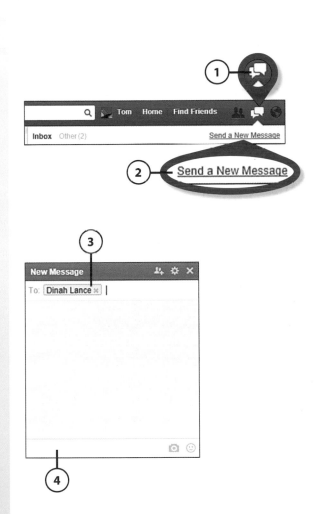

1. Click Messages on the Facebook toolbar to display the menu of options.

2. Click Send a New Message to display the New Message dialog box.

3. Enter the name of your child or grandchild into the To box.

4. Enter your message into the Write a Message box and press Enter to send the private message.

Private Messages

Learn how to send and receive private messages in Chapter 10, "Exchanging Private Messages."

Share Photos and Videos

Just as you can read each other's status updates, you can also share photos and videos with your children and grandchildren.

1. Encourage your grandkids or their parents to post photos and videos of themselves to Facebook. This provides you a constantly updated photo album of your loved ones.

2. Make sure you post the occasional photo or video of yourself, for your family members to see. Don't limit yourself to posed pictures, either; your grandkids especially will get a big kick out of any crazy or silly picture or video you upload.

Pictures and Movies

Learn more about sharing photos in Chapter 7, "Viewing and Sharing Family Photos." Learn more about sharing videos in Chapter 8, "Viewing and Sharing Home Movies."

Chat via Text and Video

If you're on one side of the country and your kids and grandkids are on the other, or even if you're only a few states away, you might only see your family in person one or two times a year. With Facebook text and video chat, you can visit with each other several times a week, if you like. It can truly bring together distant families.

① Schedule time for a weekly video chat with each of your children and grandchildren. This is especially great for talking to your younger grandkids who are sure to appreciate the one-on-one time with their favorite grandpa or grandma.

2 For the teenagers in your family, Facebook's text chat might be more up their alley. Chatting on Facebook is just like texting on a mobile phone, and you know your kids and grandkids are okay with that. Next time you're on Facebook, check to see if your favorite grandchild is also online and, if so, open a text chat and say hi. If she wants to turn it into a video chat, you always have that option.

Facebook Chat

Learn more about text and video chatting in Chapter 11, "Chatting with Friends and Family in Real Time."

Play Games Together

Here's one you might not have thought of. If your grandkids are like mine, they love to play games—board games, card games, video games, you name it. Well, Facebook is chock full of social games that you can play with other Facebook users. That means all you have to do is pick a game, and then invite your grandkids (or even your grown children) to play it with you, online.

What games are good to play with the younger members of your family? Here's a list of games to start with:

- Backgammon Live
- Chess
- Gin Rummy
- Ludo
- Monopoly: Millionaires
- Scrabble

- Smarter Than a 5th Grader?
- The Price is Right Game
- Who Wants to Be a Millionaire
- Words with Friends
- Yahtzee!

Just go to the Games Center page and search for any or all of these games by name.

Facebook Games

Learn more about finding and playing Facebook games in Chapter 15, "Playing Games."

Five Things *Not* to Do with Your Kids and Grandkids on Facebook

If your children and grandchildren are still on Facebook, you need to make sure you don't drive them away with inappropriate (for them) behavior. With that in mind, here are some important things *not* to do when posting and responding to your kids and grandkids.

1. **Don't friend their friends.** Your kids and grandkids like to keep their friends and family separate, so a family member getting friendly with one of their peers is a big social no-no. Resist the urge to send a friend request to one of your children's or grandchildren's Facebook friends. It's okay for you to accept a friend request if one of her friends invites you, but it's not okay for you to initiate the contact. In general, you should keep your circle of friends to your friends and immediate family, not to your grandchildren's friends.

2. **Don't post unflattering photos of them.** Family photos that you think are funny might not seem so funny to your kids or grandkids—especially when their friends see them. The problem comes if you upload an embarrassing photo to Facebook and tag a relative in it. Thus tagged, all her Facebook friends will see the photo, with the resulting mortification. Think twice before you post those "cute" photos, especially as they get older. And if you must post the photos, don't tag them by name. If they're not tagged, their friends probably won't see the photos—which is best for all concerned.

3. **Don't use their photo as your profile picture.** I know you're really proud of your grandkids, but you shouldn't appropriate their photos as your own. Many grandparents use photos of their grandkids as their own profile pictures, or as the cover images on their Timeline pages. That's not fair to your grandkids—and, to be fair, it looks kind of weird. Post your own photo as your profile picture, and be done with it.

4. **Don't post too much personal information.** Facebook is a great forum for keeping friends and family up-to-date on what's happening in your life, but that doesn't mean you need to post every little detail about what's happening. Your kids and grandkids, especially, will be embarrassed or even grossed out if you post all the fiddly details about your latest medical exam or (God forbid) romantic interlude. There's just some stuff that kids don't want to know, and you need to know that.

5. **Don't try to be cool.** I know, you want to fit in with the young generation today, but let's face it—you're not that young, and you're not that cool. Don't embarrass yourself by trying to use today's hip lingo, or even common Facebook abbreviations, such as LOL (laughing out loud). No matter how hip you think you might be, you'll still come off as an old fogey trying to act younger than you really are. Bottom line: When you're posting on Facebook, act your age. You've earned the privilege.

Other Places You'll Find Your Kids and Grandkids Online

So if all the hip young kids are leaving Facebook (or using it a lot less on a regular basis), where are they going? There's no one destination for your grandkids and their friends; the younger generation is splintering their time between a number of social media startups. Let's see what's out there.

Facebook-Like Social Networks

It's not surprising that many ex-Facebook users are migrating to similar post-once/read-many social media. If Facebook itself has become too broad-based, there are more targeted social media that have appeal. Here are some of the more popular social networks with younger users:

- **Ask.fm** (www.ask.fm). If your kids and grandkids have a question they need answered, they're probably turning to Ask.fm, a social media service that lets kids (and other users) ask questions and have them answered by other users—anonymously. The question-and-answer format easily leads to ongoing discussions, which the kids like.

- **Tumblr** (www.tumblr.com). Many ex-Facebook users are also migrating to Tumblr, which is kind of a cross between a traditional blog and Twitter. Tumblr users create short posts that consist of text, photos, videos, you name it, just like blog posts. Other users follow these users' *tumblelogs*, as they're called, and all posts are public. Teens and twenty-somethings use Tumblr to post personal photos, favorite videos, and random text musings. Popular posts get reblogged and often go viral. It's kind of like Twitter, but with richer content and a little less immediacy.

- **Twitter** (www.twitter.com). Twitter is a cross between an instant messaging service and a full-blown social network. Users post short (140-character max) text messages, called *tweets*, that are then broadcast publicly to that person's followers on the service. Teens like Twitter because it's short and fast and immediate, like text messaging. It's good for expressing what's on one's mind, or discovering what one's friends are up to. (It's also a great forum for keeping up with breaking news, celebrity gossip, and the like.) Twitter is probably the first alternative that most ex-Facebookers turn to.

- **Whisper** (www.whisper.sh). Whisper is a social networking app that enables users to share secrets and private thoughts publicly and anonymously. That is, users post whatever is on their minds, paired with a corresponding image. The posts are anonymous but shared publicly across the Whisper network, like the questions and answers on Ask.fm. Users can like or re-Whisper favorite posts, as well as reply to posts with posts of their own.

- **Yik Yak** (www.yikyakapp.com). Then there's Yik Yak, which is a location-aware social networking app. Users post short, anonymous text comments, which then get distributed to the 500 Yik Yak users in closest physical proximity—typically within a mile or two of the poster. This is particularly appealing to school-aged kids; whatever they post gets seen immediately by other users on campus, or even the same classroom.

Photo- and Video-Based Social Media

Many Facebook alternatives that your kids and grandkids are turning to are visual in nature. We're talking websites and apps that let people connect by sharing pictures and videos—kind of like Facebook without all those pesky words.

The most popular of these more visual social media include the following:

- **Instagram** (www.instagram.com). Instagram is the largest visual social network, period. It started as a photo app for iPhones and Android phones, complete with a series of creative "filters" that users could apply to their digital photos. (Instagram recently added the ability to shoot and share short 15-second videos, in addition to the normal picture sharing.) Teens and twenty-somethings share what they're doing by taking photos and videos and sharing them either privately with friends and followers or publicly across the entire Instagram network. Posts can be liked and shared, and photos and videos can also be cross-posted to Facebook and Twitter, which adds to the exposure.

- **Pinterest** (www.pinterest.com). Pinterest users post pictures they find on the web onto visual "pinboards," organized by topic. That results in a lot of sharing of clothing and fashion photos, crafts and do-it-yourself projects, and recipes. Women outnumber men by 4-to-1 on Pinterest, so it's a good place to connect with your daughters and nieces.

- **Snapchat** (www.snapchat.com). Younger users value their privacy, which is something that is lacking with Facebook and similar social media. Enter Snapchat, an image-based smartphone messaging app that erases all posts after they've been viewed. Users take photos and short videos with their smartphones and then post them to specific people on Snapchat. (The posts are not visible to the general public.) Each image or video is visible for a maximum of 10 seconds, and then it disappears. Nothing is stored on the recipients' devices, and nothing is stored on Snapchat's servers. It's a social network without a long-term memory. As you can imagine, that's hugely appealing to teens with short attention spans—and a proclivity toward questionable behavior.

- **Vine** (www.vine.co). Vine is kind of like Instagram for videos. (Well, Instagram lets you shoot videos now, but that was in response to Vine.) The Vine app lets you shoot looping, six-second video clips and share them publicly and with friends. It's great for sharing videos of what's happening now, but also leads to much creativity—a six-second Vine can consist of multiple shots, so there's a lot of stop-motion videos and similar fun stuff passed around. Teens share a lot of silly stuff on Vine, which makes it a fun alternative to other social media.

Mobile Messaging Media

When it comes to today's youngest users—kids under 21 or so—Facebook probably never entered into the picture. These kids started out texting on their phones and are graduating into social messaging apps that have more in common with texts than they do with Facebook posts.

These mobile messaging media are apps that enable one-to-one text messaging, but outside the traditional phone network. Sometimes the messages are text-only, sometimes they're accompanied by emoji (smiley face icons), but we're talking a more personal social network than the public networks typified by Facebook and Twitter.

Here's a sampling of the apps the younger generation is most likely to be using:

- **Kik Messenger** (www.kik.com). Kik is a smartphone app that lets users send text and photo messages to their friends and family members. It's free, has no message or character limits, and is very, very popular among the teen set.

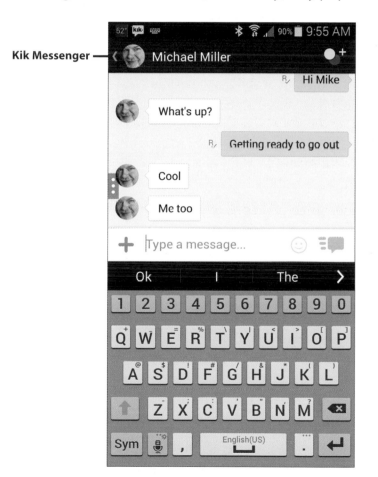

- **Oovoo** (www.oovoo.com). Oovoo is a video messaging app with serious group messaging options. The app is free and offers your choice of text, voice, and video messaging. Oovoo's big attraction is its group chatting feature, which enables users to chat with up to a dozen friends at once. It's not unusual for teens to start an Oovoo chat with a handful of classmates and keep it open while they do their homework for the evening. (Or watch TV. Or whatever.)

- **WhatsApp** (www.whatsapp.com). WhatsApp is a lot like Kik, but with text, audio, video, and photo messaging. People can use their smartphones to send messages to single recipients or groups of friends, with free unlimited messaging. In other words, it's a great alternative for kids who push up against the limits of the phone company's standard text messaging plans.

Youngsters Only?

I'll be honest. You won't find a lot of people aged 50 and up on most of these newer social networks—which is why they're so appealing to younger users. Still, if you know your kids and grandkids are big on Twitter or Instagram and you want to stay in touch, you might want to investigate.

Privacy Shortcuts button

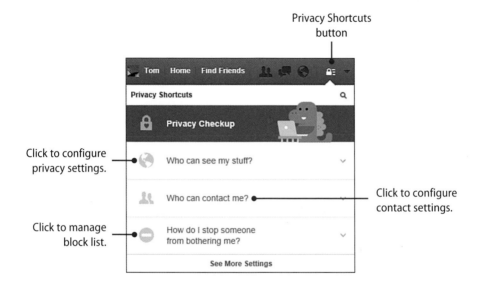

Click to configure privacy settings.

Click to configure contact settings.

Click to manage block list.

In this chapter, you find out how to keep your private information from becoming public on the Facebook site.

→ Determining Who Sees What You Post
→ Limiting Contact from Other Members
→ Controlling Tagging
→ Controlling Who Sees What on Your Timeline

Managing Your Privacy on Facebook

Facebook is a social network, and being social means sharing one's personal information with others. In Facebook's case, it's likely that you're sharing a lot of your private information not just with your friends but also with Facebook and its partners and advertisers.

Unfortunately, all this sharing poses a problem if you'd rather keep some things private. If you share everything with everyone, all sorts of information can get out—and be seen by people you don't want to see it. Keeping personal information personal on Facebook is possible, but it requires some work on your part.

Determining Who Sees What You Post

Many people worry about their privacy online, and for good reason. Not only are there a lot of companies that would like to get hold of your private information to contact you for advertising and promotional reasons, but the Internet is also rife with identify thieves eager to steal your private information for their own nefarious means.

This is why some people are cautious about getting on Facebook; they're afraid that the information they post will be needlessly shared with the wrong people. There's a basis to these fears, as Facebook likes to share all your information with just about everybody on its social network—not just your friends or their friends, but also advertisers and third-party websites.

Fortunately, you can configure Facebook to be much less public than it could be—and thus keep your private information private. You just have to know which settings to tweak.

Configure Facebook's Default Privacy Settings

The first step to ensuring your Facebook privacy is to determine who, by default, can see all the posts you make. You can do this in a positive fashion, by telling Facebook precisely who can view your new posts. You can also take a more defensive approach, by telling Facebook who *can't* see your status updates.

Default Sharing

Facebook's default sharing settings used to be Public, meaning that all your information and status updates were shared with everyone. Fortunately, that's not the case anymore. Today, Facebook sets the default sharing setting for all new users as Friends, meaning your posts and profile information are visible only to those users on your friends list. (If you signed up for Facebook prior to May 2014, your default privacy setting is probably still set as Public.)

(1) Click the Privacy Shortcuts button on the Facebook toolbar to display the pull-down menu.

(2) Click the down arrow next to Who Can See My Stuff? to expand the menu.

(3) Go to the Who Can See My Future Posts? section, click the down arrow, and select one of the resulting options.

(4) Click Public to let anyone on Facebook see your posts.

(5) Click Friends to restrict viewing to only people on your Facebook friends list.

(6) Click More Options to further expand the menu.

(7) Click Only Me to keep your posts totally private—that is, to keep anyone from seeing them.

(8) Click Custom to create a custom list of people who can or can't see your posts. The Custom Privacy panel displays.

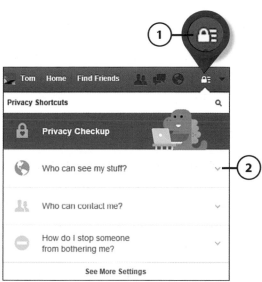

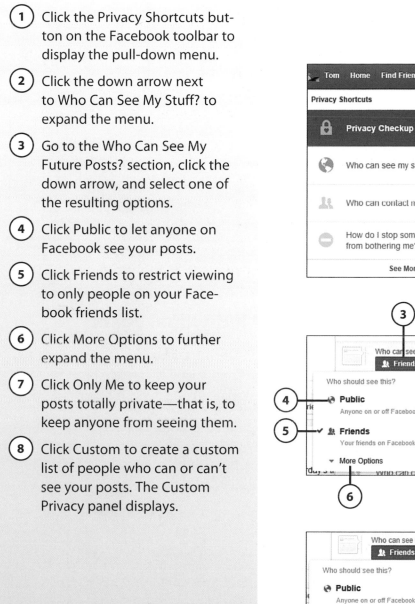

(9) In the Share This With box, enter the names of friends or groups of friends you want to share with.

(10) To share with friends of people you tag in your posts or photos, check the Friends of Tagged option.

(11) To *not* share your posts with a given friend or group of friends, enter that name into the Don't Share This With box.

(12) Click the Save Changes button.

Custom Privacy

+ **Share this with**

These people or lists   Friends ✕

Friends of tagged   ✓

Note: Anyone tagged can also see this post.

✕ **Don't share this with**

These people or lists

Cancel   Save Changes

Select Who Can See (or Not See) Individual Posts

Even after you set these global posting privacy settings, you can change the privacy setting for any individual post you make. That is, any given post can be sent to a specific list of people that overrides the global settings you made previously.

For example, you might have set your global privacy settings so that your friends can see your posts. But if you have a new post that you only want your immediate family to see, you can configure that single post to go only to your family members, not to everyone else on your friends list.

(1) Go to your Facebook Home page and start a new status update as normal.

(2) Click the Post Privacy Setting button to display the menu of options.

(3) Click Public to make this post visible to any Facebook user.

Update Status   Add Photos/Video

What's on your mind?

👤 📍 📷 🙂   **👥 Friends ▾**   **Post**

Who should see this?

Tom French
Just now · 👤▾

Missing all of you!

🌐 **Public**
Anyone on or off Facebook

✓ 👥 **Friends**
Your friends on Facebook

▾ **More Options**

4 Click Friends to make this post visible to everyone on your friends list.

5 Click More Options to further expand the menu.

6 Click Only Me to keep your posts totally private—that is, to keep anyone from seeing them.

7 Click Custom to display the Custom Privacy panel, and then specify the people who can see this post.

8 Select the necessary options to make this post visible to or hide it from specific people or groups of friends.

9 Click the Save Changes button. This new setting applies for all future posts—until you change it again.

Limiting Contact from Other Members

Are you getting private messages or friend requests from people you don't know? It's time to reconfigure your privacy settings to limit contact from complete strangers.

Control Who Can Contact You

By default, just about anybody who Facebook thinks you might know can send you private messages. If you'd rather not be contacted by complete strangers, you can tell Facebook to let only your friends send you messages.

(1) From the Facebook toolbar, click the Privacy Shortcuts button to display the drop-down menu.

(2) Click the down arrow next to Who Can Contact Me? to expand this section.

(3) Basic Filtering is selected by default. Select Strict Filtering to see private messages from only people on your friends list.

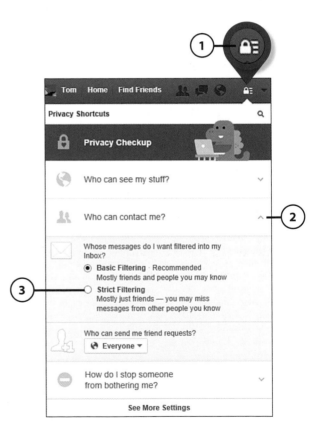

Control Who Can Send You Friend Requests

You can also limit who on Facebook can request to be your friend. By default, anyone on Facebook can friend you; you might not want to see friend requests from people you don't know, however.

(1) From the Facebook toolbar, click the Privacy Shortcuts button to display the drop-down menu.

(2) Click the down arrow next to Who Can Contact Me? to expand this section.

(3) Go to the Who Can Send Me Friend Requests? section and click the Privacy button. (By default, the button says "Everyone.")

(4) Click Friends of Friends to limit friend requests to people who know the people you know—people who are friends with your Facebook friends.

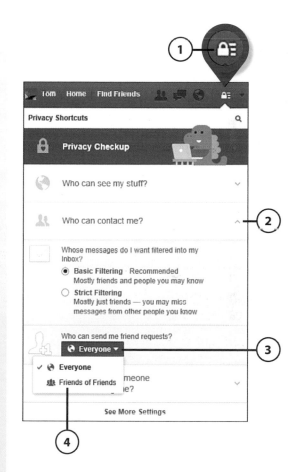

Controlling Tagging

Facebook likes to connect people with each other. This is often done via "tagging," where one user can tag ("who are you with?") another user in a status update or photo without asking the other person. When you're tagged, you're connected to that post or photo, whether you want to be or not—which can be an invasion of your privacy.

Restrict Who Sees Tag Suggestions in Photos That Look Like You

One of the ways that Facebook encourages tagging is by suggesting people to tag when someone posts a photo. Facebook does this via facial recognition technology; it compares a given photo with the millions of other photos uploaded to its site and tries to match a new face with one it already knows.

So if someone uploads a picture of someone who looks like you, Facebook suggests that you be tagged in that photo. That's fine, unless that's not really you—or if the photo is one you'd rather not be associated with. Fortunately, you can turn off these photo tag suggestions.

It's Not All Good

You Can Still Be Tagged

Just because you turn off Facebook's ability to suggest your name when someone uploads a photo, that doesn't mean you can't be tagged in that photo. The person who uploaded the photo can still manually tag you, even if your name isn't automatically suggested.

1. From the Facebook toolbar, click the down arrow button to display the menu of options.

2. Click Settings to display the Account Settings page.

3. Click Timeline and Tagging in the left-hand column to display the Timeline and Tagging Settings page.

4. Go to the How Can I Manage Tags People Add and Tagging Suggestions? section.

5. Go to the Who Sees Tag Suggestions When Photos That Look Like You Are Uploaded? option and click Edit.

6. Click the Privacy button to see the list of options.

7. By default, Friends is selected, which means that all of your friends will see your name in their tag suggestions. Click No One to keep your name from appearing as a tag suggestion for anyone, including your friends.

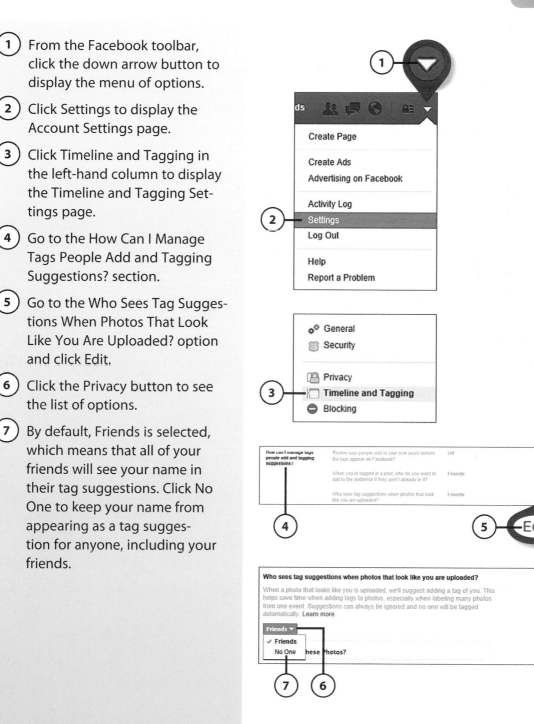

Limit Who Can See Posts You're Tagged In

As noted, there's nothing to stop friends from manually tagging you in the posts they make and the photos they upload. What you can do, however, is keep anyone else from seeing those tags—in effect, hiding your name when tagged.

1. From the Facebook toolbar, click the down arrow button to display the menu of options.

2. Click Settings to display the Account Settings page.

3. Click Timeline and Tagging in the left-hand column to display the Timeline and Tagging Settings page.

4. Go to the Who Can See Things on My Timeline? section.

5. Go to the Who Can See Posts You've Been Tagged In On Your Timeline? option and click Edit.

6. Click the Privacy button to display the list of options.

7. Click Friends to limit your exposure to only people on your friends list.

8. Click Only Me to hide your name from everyone on Facebook.

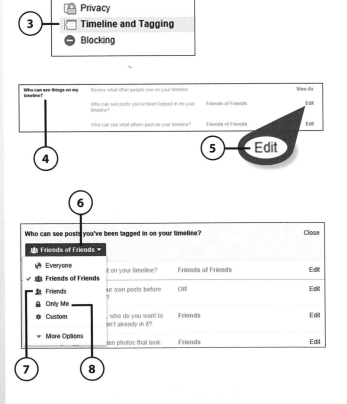

Approve Tags People Add to Your Posts

Here's a real invasion of your privacy. You post a picture to Facebook, and someone tags himself in your photo—even if it's not really a picture of him! Fortunately, Facebook gives you the option of reviewing all tags that people add to the posts you make and the photos you upload—so you can restrict who "associates" with you online.

1. From the Facebook toolbar, click the down arrow button to display the menu of options.

2. Click Settings to display the Account Settings page.

3. Click Timeline and Tagging in the left-hand column to display the Timeline and Tagging Settings page.

4. Go to the How Can I Manage Tags People Add and Tagging Suggestions? section.

5. Go to the Review Tags People Add to Your Own Posts Before the Tags Appear on Facebook? option and click Edit.

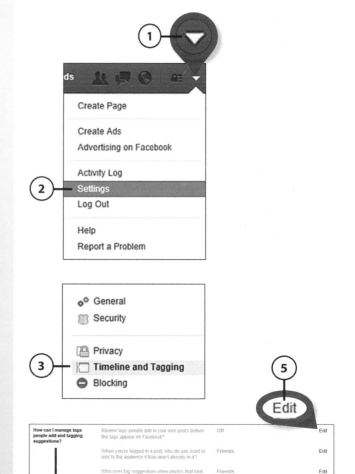

6 Click the Privacy button to see the list of options.

7 Click Enabled. You are notified whenever someone tries to add his or her tag to one of your posts or photos, and you have the option of approving or rejecting that tag.

Controlling Who Sees What on Your Timeline

Another place that Facebook displays personal information is on your Timeline. Fortunately, you can limit who can see specific information there—and hide entire sections, if you like.

Control Who Sees Specific Information

Any given section in your Timeline has its own privacy settings. That is, you can configure different parts of your Timeline to be visible to different groups of people. For example, you can configure your Timeline so that everyone on Facebook can see your About section, but limit viewing of your Photos section to only people on your friends list.

1 Click your name on the toolbar to display your Timeline page.

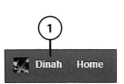

2 Click the Update Info button.

 Update Info   View Activity Log 1 ...

2

3 In the left column, select the type of information you want to configure.

4 Mouse over the individual item you want to change, and then click that item's Privacy button.

5 Select who can see this information: Public (everyone on Facebook), Friends (people on your friends list), Only Me (no one can see it), Custom, or one of your customized friends lists.

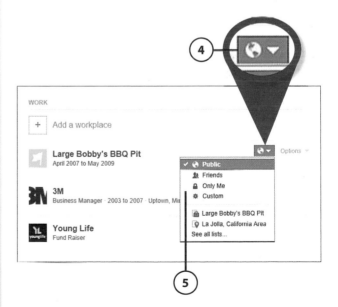

Hide Sections of Your Timeline

In addition to setting privacy options for individual pieces of information, you can also choose to hide entire sections of your Timeline. For example, if you don't want anyone to see the Places you've been or Music you've listened to, you can hide those sections.

 1 Click your name on the toolbar to display your Timeline page.

2 Click the Edit (pencil) button for the section you want to hide.

3 Click Hide Section.

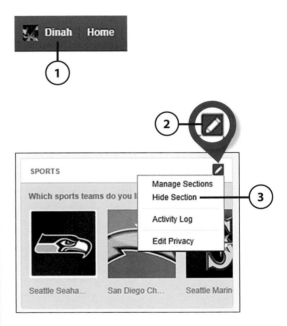

General account
settings

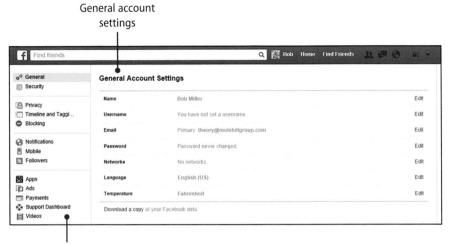

Type of settings to
configure

In this chapter, you learn how to configure various aspects of your Facebook account.

→ Changing Your Account Settings
→ Leaving Facebook
→ Dealing with Death

Managing Your Facebook Account

Your Facebook account contains your basic personal information—your name, email address, password, and the like. What do you do if you move, get a new email account, or find that your password is compromised? Fortunately, Facebook lets you easily change any and all of this information, at any time.

Changing Your Account Settings

You can change all your Facebook settings from the Account Settings page, which you access from the Facebook toolbar. The Account Settings page has a dozen or so different tabs, each of which hosts a specific type of information.

Configure General Account Settings

When you want to change your Facebook username, email address, or password, select the General Account Settings tab.

1. Click the down arrow on the far right of the Facebook toolbar to display the menu of options.

2. Click Settings to display the Account Settings page.

3. Click the General tab in the left column to display the General Account Settings.

4. Click Edit in the Name section to change your name on Facebook.

5. Click Edit in the Username section to set or change your official Facebook username.

6. Click Edit in the Email section to change the email address you've linked to your Facebook account.

7. Click Edit in the Password section to change your Facebook password.

Changing Passwords

It's a good idea to change your Facebook password every month or two. This decreases the possibility of your account password being hacked.

8 Click Edit in the Networks section to manage any school or work networks you have.

Networks

A Facebook network is like a group for people who attended a specific school or worked at a given company. To join a network, you must have an official email address from that school or company (for example, if you work at 3M and have a *yourname*@3m.com email address).

9 Click Edit in the Language section to change the language in which you read Facebook.

10 Click Edit in the Temperature section to change from Fahrenheit to Celsius when displaying current temperature on the site.

General Account Settings

Name	Bob Miller	Edit
Username	You have not set a username	Edit
Email	Primary: theory@molehillgroup.com	Edit
Password	Password never changed	Edit
Networks	No networks	Edit
Language	English (US)	Edit
Temperature	Fahrenheit	Edit

Download a copy of your Facebook data

Configure Security Settings

To change settings related to your system security, select the Security tab. You can also deactivate your Facebook account from this page.

1 Click the down arrow on the far right of the Facebook toolbar to display the menu of options.

2 Click Settings to display the Account Settings page.

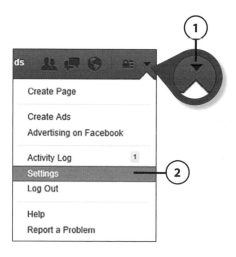

Create Page

Create Ads

Advertising on Facebook

Activity Log

Settings

Log Out

Help

Report a Problem

3 Click the Security tab in the left column to display the Security Settings.

4 Click Edit in the Login Notifications section if you want to be notified when your Facebook account is accessed from a computer or mobile device that you haven't used before.

5 Click Edit in the Login Approvals section to set up two-step authentication, which entails sending a security code to your mobile phone when Facebook is opened on an unknown web browser.

6 Click Edit in the Code Generator section to generate security codes from within the Facebook mobile app.

7 Click Edit in the App Passwords section to manage passwords you use for various Facebook apps.

8 Click Edit in the Trusted Contacts section to set some of your friends as "trusted contacts" who can help you reset your password if you can't log in.

9 Click Edit in the Trusted Browsers section to review which web browsers you've saved as your most often used.

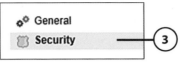

Security Settings

Login Notifications	Get notified when it looks like someone else is trying to access your account.	Edit
Login Approvals	Use your phone as an extra layer of security to keep other people from logging into your account.	Edit
Code Generator	Use your Facebook app to get security codes when you need them.	Edit
App Passwords	Use special passwords to log into your apps instead of using your Facebook password or Login Approvals codes.	Edit
Trusted Contacts	Pick friends you can call to help you get back into your account if you get locked out.	Edit
Trusted Browsers	Review which browsers you saved as ones you often use.	Edit
Where You're Logged In	Review and manage where you're currently logged into Facebook.	Edit

Deactivate your account.

10 Click Edit in the Where You're Logged In section to view the most recent locations from which you've logged into Facebook.

Active Sessions

If you think someone else has been logging into your Facebook account without your knowledge, use the Where You're Logged In list to compare Facebook's login records with what you know you've done.

Security Settings

Login Notifications	Get notified when it looks like someone else is trying to access your account.	Edit
Login Approvals	Use your phone as an extra layer of security to keep other people from logging into your account.	Edit
Code Generator	Use your Facebook app to get security codes when you need them.	Edit
App Passwords	Use special passwords to log into your apps instead of using your Facebook password or Login Approvals codes.	Edit
Trusted Contacts	Pick friends you can call to help you get back into your account if you get locked out	Edit
Trusted Browsers	Review which browsers you saved as ones you often use	Edit
Where You're Logged In	Review and manage where you're currently logged into Facebook.	Edit
Deactivate your account.		

10

Configure Privacy Settings

Chapter 18, "Managing Your Privacy on Facebook," covers several of Facebook's privacy settings. You can access many of these same settings from the Account Settings page.

1 Click the down arrow on the far right of the Facebook toolbar to display the menu of options.

2 Click Settings to display the Account Settings page.

3 Click the Privacy tab in the left column to display the Privacy Settings and Tools page.

4 Click Edit in the Who Can See Your Future Posts? section to configure who can view your status updates.

5 Click Use Activity Log to use the Activity Log to review all your posts and items in which you've been tagged.

6 Click Limit Past Posts to limit viewing of your previous posts to only those people on your friends list.

7 Click Edit in the Who Can Send You Friend Requests? section to limit who can send you friend requests on Facebook.

8 Click Edit in the Whose Messages Do I Want Filtered Into My Inbox? section to limit who can send you private messages.

9 Click Edit in the Who Can Look You Up Using the Email Address You Provided? section to limit who can look you up on Facebook via email address.

10 Click Edit in the Who Can Look You Up Using the Phone Number You Provided? section to limit who can look you up on Facebook via your phone number.

11 Click Edit in the Do You Want Other Search Engines to Link to Your Timeline? section if you'd rather not have your Facebook information searchable via Google and other search engines.

Privacy Settings and Tools

Who can see my stuff?	Who can see your future posts?	Friends	Edit
	Review all your posts and things you're tagged in		Use Activity Log
	Limit the audience for posts you've shared with friends of friends or Public?		Limit Past Posts
Who can contact me?	Who can send you friend requests?	Everyone	Edit
	Whose messages do I want filtered into my Inbox?	Strict Filtering	Edit
Who can look me up?	Who can look you up using the email address you provided?	Everyone	Edit
	Who can look you up using the phone number you provided?	Everyone	Edit
	Do you want other search engines to link to your timeline?	Yes	Edit

Privacy Settings and Tools

Who can see my stuff?	Who can see your future posts?	Friends	Edit
	Review all your posts and things you're tagged in		Use Activity Log
	Limit the audience for posts you've shared with friends of friends or Public?		Limit Past Posts
Who can contact me?	Who can send you friend requests?	Everyone	Edit
	Whose messages do I want filtered into my Inbox?	Strict Filtering	Edit
Who can look me up?	Who can look you up using the email address you provided?	Everyone	Edit
	Who can look you up using the phone number you provided?	Everyone	Edit
	Do you want other search engines to link to your timeline?	Yes	Edit

Configure Timeline and Tagging Settings

To determine who can add things to or see items on your Timeline, use the Timeline and Tagging page.

1. Click the down arrow on the far right of the Facebook toolbar to display the menu of options.

2. Click Settings to display the Account Settings page.

3. Click the Timeline and Tagging tab in the left column to display the Timeline and Tagging Settings.

4. Click Edit in the Who Can Post on Your Timeline? section to control who can post messages to your Timeline page.

5. Click Edit in the Review Posts Friends Tag You in Before They Appear on Your Timeline? section to manually approve any posts or photos in which you've been tagged.

6. Click View As in the Review What Other People See On Your Timeline section to display your Timeline as it's seen by other users.

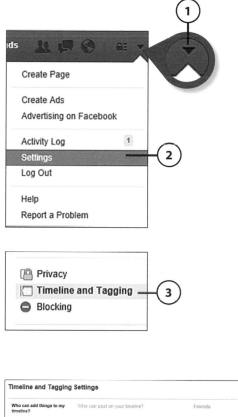

(7) Click Edit in the Who Can See Posts You've Been Tagged In On Your Timeline? section to determine who can see posts or photos in which you've been tagged.

(8) Click Edit in the Who Can See What Others Post on Your Timeline? section to determine who can see posts that others make on your Timeline.

(9) Click Edit in the Review Tags People Add to Your Own Posts Before the Tags Appear on Facebook? to manually approve any tags that people add to your posts or photos.

(10) Click Edit in the When You're Tagged in a Post, Who Do You Want to Add to the Audience If They Aren't Already In It? section to display items in which you've been tagged to other users.

(11) Click Edit in the Who Sees Tag Suggestions When Photos That Look Like You Are Uploaded? section to determine who can see your name in the tag selections for pictures they've uploaded.

Timeline and Tagging Settings

Who can add things to my timeline?	Who can post on your timeline?	Friends	Edit
	Review posts friends tag you in before they appear on your timeline?	Off	Edit
Who can see things on my timeline?	Review what other people see on your timeline		View As
	Who can see posts you've been tagged in on your timeline?	Friends of Friends	Edit
	Who can see what others post on your timeline?	Friends of Friends	Edit
How can I manage tags people add and tagging suggestions?	Review tags people add to your own posts before the tags appear on Facebook?	Off	Edit
	When you're tagged in a post, who do you want to add to the audience if they aren't already in it?	Friends	Edit
	Who sees tag suggestions when photos that look like you are uploaded?	Friends	Edit

Manage Blocked Users

Facebook enables you to block users who are annoying you; when someone is blocked, they're added to your Restricted list and nothing they write ever gets to you. You can also block messages from annoying apps. Just use the Blocking page.

(1) Click the down arrow on the far right of the Facebook toolbar to display the menu of options.

(2) Click Settings to display the Account Settings page.

(3) Click the Blocking tab in the left column to display the Manage Blocking page.

(4) Click Edit List in the Restricted List section to add or remove friends from your Restricted list. (Friends on your Restricted list only see your posts that are defined as Public, not those restricted to friends only.)

(5) To add a friend to the Restricted list, click the button at the top-left corner of the panel and select Friends. Click the person's name and click the Finish button.

6 To completely block a person from seeing your posts or contacting you, go to the Block Users section, enter that person's name, and then click Block.

7 Block app invitations from a specific user by going to the Block App Invites section, entering his or her name into the Block Invites From box, and pressing Enter.

8 Block event invitations from a specific user by going to the Block Event Invites section, entering his or her name into the Block Invites From box, and pressing Enter.

9 Keep a given app or game from contacting you on Facebook by going to the Block Apps section, entering the name of that app into the Block Apps box, and pressing Enter.

10 Block interaction with Pages you've previously liked by going to the Block Pages section, entering the name of that Page into the Block Pages box, and pressing enter.

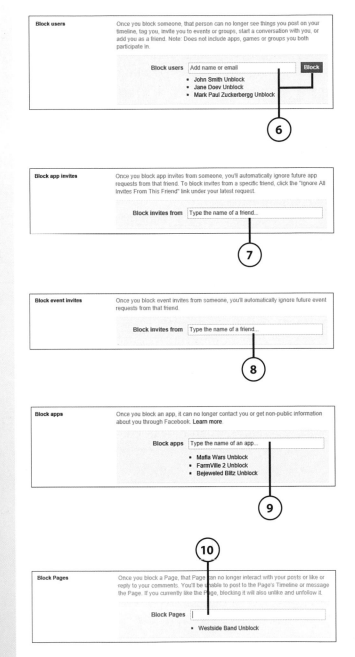

Block users — Once you block someone, that person can no longer see things you post on your timeline, tag you, invite you to events or groups, start a conversation with you, or add you as a friend. Note: Does not include apps, games or groups you both participate in.

Block users: Add name or email **Block**
- John Smith Unblock
- Jane Doev Unblock
- Mark Paul Zuckerbergg Unblock

Block app invites — Once you block app invites from someone, you'll automatically ignore future app requests from that friend. To block invites from a specific friend, click the "Ignore All Invites From This Friend" link under your latest request.

Block invites from: Type the name of a friend...

Block event invites — Once you block event invites from someone, you'll automatically ignore future event requests from that friend.

Block invites from: Type the name of a friend...

Block apps — Once you block an app, it can no longer contact you or get non-public information about you through Facebook. Learn more.

Block apps: Type the name of an app...
- Mafia Wars Unblock
- FarmVille 2 Unblock
- Bejeweled Blitz Unblock

Block Pages — Once you block a Page, that Page can no longer interact with your posts or like or reply to your comments. You'll be unable to post to the Page's Timeline or message the Page. If you currently like the Page, blocking it will also unlike and unfollow it.

Block Pages:
- Westside Band Unblock

Configure Notifications

Facebook gladly notifies you of all sorts of activity related to your account—when a friend makes a post, when you get tagged in a post or photo, or even when someone posts to one of the groups to which you belong. You can opt to get notified on Facebook or via email or text message.

1. Click the down arrow on the far right of the Facebook toolbar to display the menu of options.

2. Click Settings to display the Account Settings page.

3. Click the Notifications tab in the left column to display the Notifications Settings page.

4. Click View in the On Facebook section to turn off the sound Facebook makes when you receive a new notification.

5. Click Edit in the Email section to determine what types of notifications you receive via email.

6. Click View in the Push Notifications section to view which apps can send notifications to your mobile phone.

7. Click Edit in the Text Message section to determine what types of notifications you receive via text message to your mobile phone.

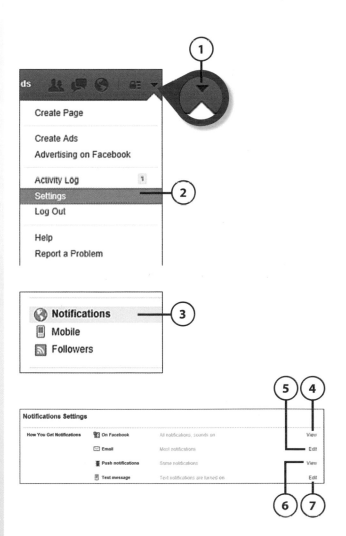

8. Click Edit for activities listed in the What You Get Notified About section to determine which activities you receive notifications about.

What You Get Notified About	Activity that involves you	On	View
	Close Friends activity	On Facebook and Email	Edit
	Birthdays	On	Edit
	Your friends' life events	On	Edit
	Tags	Anyone	Edit
	Followers	On for Friends of Friends	Edit
	Group activity	On for 2 of your 6 groups	Edit
	App requests and activity	On for 11 of your 11 apps	Edit

Configure Facebook for Mobile Use

Many users opt to send new status updates to Facebook via text message from their phones. To do this, you must register your mobile phone number with Facebook.

1. Click the down arrow on the far right of the Facebook toolbar to display the menu of options.

2. Click Settings to display the Account Settings page.

3. Click the Mobile tab in the left column to display the Mobile Settings page.

Create Page

Create Ads
Advertising on Facebook

Activity Log 1
Settings
Log Out

Help
Report a Problem

Notifications
Mobile
Followers

4 Click the Add a Phone button to display the Activate Facebook Texts dialog box to register your mobile phone with Facebook.

5 Select the country of your mobile phone carrier from the Country/Region list.

6 Select your mobile phone carrier from the Mobile Carrier list.

7 Click the Next button.

8 From your mobile phone, text the letter F to 32665 (FBOOK).

9 Facebook sends a confirmation code via text message to your mobile phone. Enter that code into the Confirmation Code box.

10 Uncheck the Share My Phone Number with My Friends box if you don't want your Facebook friends to see your mobile phone number.

11 Uncheck the Allow Friends to Text Me from Facebook box if you don't want friends to text you via Facebook.

12 Click the Next button to display the Mobile Settings page.

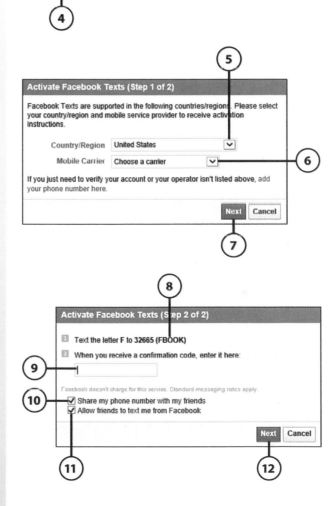

(13) Click Edit in the Text Messaging section if you've already registered your mobile phone number and want to change it.

(14) By default, Facebook texts you when anyone posts a message for you from his mobile phone. To not receive these texts, click Edit in the Facebook Messages section and make a new selection from the Text Me list.

(15) Click Edit in the Daily Text Limit section and choose a quantity to limit the number of daily text messages that Facebook can send you.

(16) To send a status update via email message, text the message to the email address displayed in the Post-By-Email Address section.

Text Messaging	Send texts to: (612) ••• ••••	Edit
Facebook Messages	Text me: When someone sends me a Message on web or mobile	Edit
Daily Text Limit	Maximum number of texts: Unlimited	Edit
Post-By-Email Address	••• •••••• @m.facebook.com	Edit

Manage Following and Followers

If you have a lot of people who want to read your status updates but you don't necessarily want to read theirs, you can activate Facebook's Following feature. With Following activated, others can opt to follow your posts without having to be on your friends list.

Following

Following is best suited for public people or organizations with a large number of fans or customers, not for regular individuals.

(1) Click the down arrow on the far right of the Facebook toolbar to display the menu of options.

(2) Click Settings to display the Account Settings page.

(3) Click the Followers tab in the left column to display the Follower Settings page.

(4) In the Who Can Follow Me section, click the button to select who can follow you—Everybody or just Friends.

(5) Click Edit in the Follower Comments section to determine whether or not followers can comment on your posts.

(6) Click Edit in the Follower Notifications section to receive notifications when people who aren't your friends start following you.

(7) Click Edit in the Username section to change the username that followers see.

(8) Click Edit in the Twitter section to connect your Facebook account to your Twitter account, so that one post goes to both social networks.

(9) If you run your own website and want to add a Facebook Follow button to your site, copy the code in the Follow Plugin section to the desired web page.

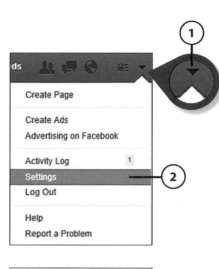

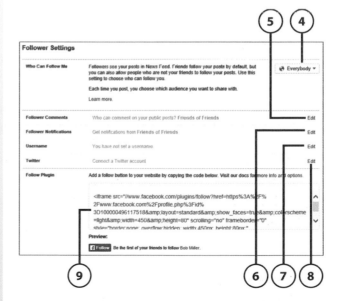

Manage Apps and Games

If you use a lot of Facebook apps or games, you can edit how those apps interact with your Facebook account. You can even delete unused apps, if you want, so they won't bother you with unwanted notifications.

(1) Click the down arrow on the far right of the Facebook toolbar to display the menu of options.

(2) Click Settings to display the Account Settings page.

(3) Click the Apps tab in the left column to display the App Settings page.

(4) Mouse over an app or game and click the Edit Settings button to edit the settings for that app.

(5) To delete an app, mouse over that app and click the Remove (X) button; when prompted, click the Remove button.

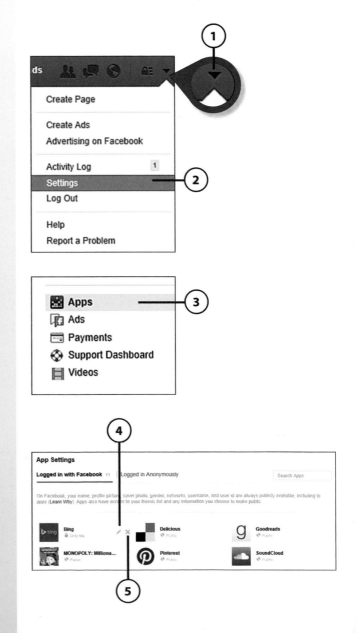

6 To turn off all integration between your Facebook account and other websites, go to the Apps, Websites and Plugins section, click the Edit button, and then click Disable Platform.

7 Some websites use your friends' Facebook data to present a more personalized experience when you visit their sites. To turn off this sharing of data (which some find a bit creepy), go to the Instant Personalization section, click Edit, and then click Disable Instant Personalization.

8 To limit which information your friends' apps can use, go to the Apps Others Use section and click the Edit button. You now see a panel that lists all the different types of personal information; uncheck those you don't want to share.

9 If you're using an older version of Facebook's mobile app and want to better control the privacy of the information posted there, go to the Old Versions of Facebook for Mobile, click the Privacy button, and select who can see this old information. (You probably don't need to worry about this one.)

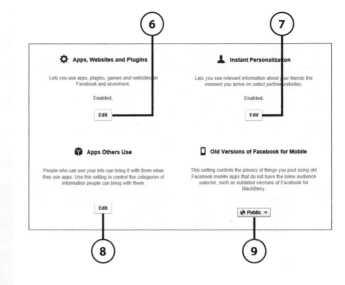

Configure Ad Settings

Some advertisers like to use information you provide to Facebook to provide more personal ads to your friends. These ads typically say something like "John Doe likes this page" or product or whatever. Some people don't like being used by advertisers without just compensation (which they don't provide); for this reason, Facebook enables you to control how advertisers can use your information.

(1) Click the down arrow on the far right of the Facebook toolbar to display the menu of options.

(2) Click Settings to display the Account Settings page.

(3) Click the Ads tab in the left column to display the Facebook Ads page.

(4) At present Facebook does not let third-party advertisers use your name or picture in their non-Facebook ads. If Facebook changes this policy, you can tell Facebook *not* to use your information in this manner by clicking Edit in the Third Party Sites section, and then selecting No One from the list.

(5) To prohibit advertisers from linking your name to their products in Facebook ads presented to your friends, click Edit in the Ads and Friends section, and then select No One from the list.

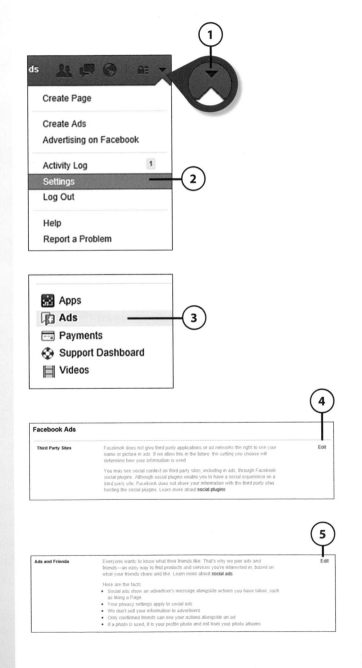

Manage Facebook Payments

Some Facebook apps and games let you purchase additional items from within that environment. You can pay for your in-game and in-app purchases with Facebook's own proprietary transaction process service, dubbed Facebook Payments. This service works much like PayPal, in that it enables you to pay via credit card from within Facebook. You can manage your Facebook Payments account on the Payments tab.

1. Click the down arrow button on the far right of the Facebook toolbar to display the menu of options.

2. Click Settings to display the Account Settings page.

3. Click the Payments tab in the left column to display the Payments Settings page.

4. Your current account balance is displayed in the Account Balance section near the top of the page content.

5. Click View in the Subscriptions section to view any recurring subscription payments you've set up.

6 Click View in the Purchase History section to examine your recent purchase history.

7 Click Manage in the Payment Methods section to manage your payment methods (credit card and so forth).

8 Click Edit in the Preferred Currency section to change the currency you use.

9 Click Manage in the Shipping Addresses to add and manage your shipping address for any physical purchases you make via Facebook.

Payments Settings

Account Balance		0 [¥]
Subscriptions	You have 0 recurring payments set up for apps on Facebook.	View
Purchase History	View your recent purchases.	View
Payment Methods	You do not have any payment methods saved.	Manage
Preferred Currency	Currencies will be shown and purchased as US Dollar	Edit
Shipping Addresses	You do not have any addresses saved.	Manage

Configure Video Playback Options

More and more people are uploading videos to Facebook. You can configure how these videos play on your system.

1 Click the down arrow button on the far right of the Facebook toolbar to display the menu of options.

2 Click Settings to display the Account Settings page.

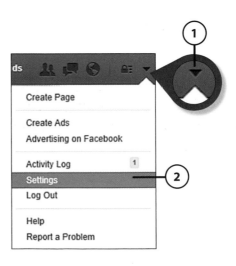

Create Page
Create Ads
Advertising on Facebook
Activity Log   1
Settings
Log Out
Help
Report a Problem

3 Click the Videos tab in the left column to display the Video Settings page.

Apps
Ads
Payments
Support Dashboard
Videos ———————— **3**

4 To determine the quality of the video playback—standard definition (SD), high definition (HD), or automatic—click the Video Default Quality (Default) button and make a selection.

4

Video Settings

| Video Default Quality | You can still change the quality of a video you are watching by clicking the HD icon in the video player. | Default ▼ |
| Auto-Play Videos | These settings only apply when you use the Facebook website. Follow this guide to change auto-play videos in your Facebook app. | On ▼ |

5 By default, many videos start playing automatically when you scroll to them in your News Feed. To turn off this automatic playback, click the Auto-Play Videos button and select Off.

5

Leaving Facebook

If you ever choose to leave Facebook, you have two options. You can *deactivate* your account, which temporarily hides your account information from others, or you can *delete* your account, which permanently removes your account information.

Deactivate Your Account

Deactivating your account is meant as a temporary solution that you can undo at any future point. When you deactivate your account, Facebook doesn't actually delete your account information; it merely hides it so others can't view it. Because your account information still exists, it's simple enough to reactivate a deactivated account.

1. Click the down arrow on the far right of the Facebook toolbar to display the menu of options.

2. Click Settings to display the Account Settings page.

3. Click the Security tab in the left column to display the Security Settings page.

4. Scroll to the bottom of the page and click Deactivate Your Account to display the Are You Sure You Want to Deactivate Your Account? page.

5. Scroll to the Reason for Leaving section and select just why it is you're leaving. This is a requirement; you have to tell Facebook something here.

6. Check the Email Opt Out box if you don't want to be hounded by Facebook to venture back into the fold.

7. Click the Confirm button to deactivate your account.

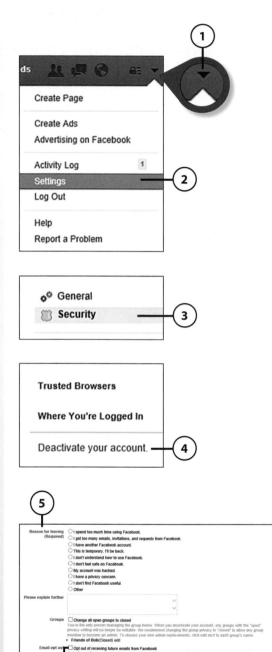

They'll Miss You!

Facebook really, really doesn't want to see you leave, so it tugs at your heartstrings by showing you pictures of some of your Facebook friends with the messages "Bob will miss you," "Dinah will miss you," and so forth. If you truly want to leave, resist the urge to change your mind.

Permanently Delete Your Facebook Account

If you're absolutely, positively sure you'll never want to be a Facebook user again—and you want more reassurance that your personal data has been wiped—then you want to permanently delete your account. This is more difficult to do than deactivating your account for the simple reason that your Facebook account is likely connected to lots of other websites.

It's Not All Good

It's Final

Deleting your Facebook account is final; all your status updates and other information will be permanently erased. If you later want to rejoin Facebook, you'll have to start completely from scratch.

(1) Go to each website you've linked to your Facebook account and disconnect the link—that is, create a new login ID that is not related to your Facebook ID. Do *not* log into these sites with your Facebook account!

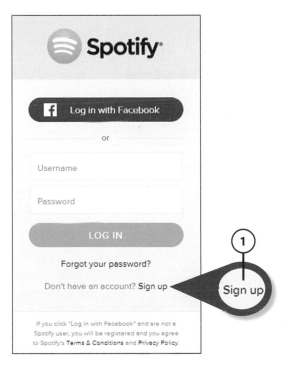

(2) Log in to your Facebook account and go to Facebook's Delete My Account page (www.facebook.com/help/delete_account). You have to enter this URL directly into your web browser; there's no link to this page from within Facebook.

(3) Click the Delete My Account button to display the Permanently Delete Account dialog box.

(4) Enter your Facebook password into the Password box.

(5) Enter the displayed characters into the Security Check box.

(6) Click the OK button.

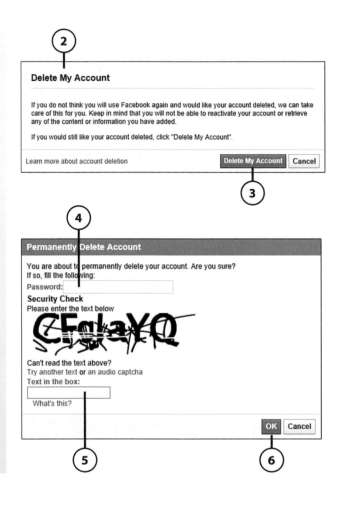

It's Not All Good

14 Days

When you follow this procedure, Facebook deletes your account—so long as you don't log back in to Facebook or log onto any websites that you log into with your Facebook account for the next 14 days. Any interaction with your Facebook account during this 14-day period reactivates your account. This also means not clicking the Facebook Like button on any other website.

Dealing with Death

Here's a question none of us want to face but all of us will have to: What happens to your Facebook account when you die?

The legal status of one's online accounts is a growing issue as online users age. After all, only you are supposed to have access to your online accounts; only you know your password to get into Facebook, Twitter, or even your online banking site (although you could share these with a loved one, for security purposes). And if you aren't able to get online, because you're dead, how can your accounts be put on hold or deleted?

Facebook, fortunately, has considered this situation and offers several options for accounts belonging to deceased members: You can memorialize the account, or you can simply remove it from the Facebook site.

Memorialize an Account

If you choose to memorialize the deceased's account, Facebook retains that person's Timeline page but locks it so that no one can log into it, and so no new friends can be accepted. Current friends, however, can share memories of the deceased on the memorialized timeline, and all existing content remains available for friends to view. (Who can view it depends on the Timeline's existing privacy settings.)

Anyone can report a deceased user to Facebook, and thus begin the memorialization process.

(1) From your web browser, go to www.facebook.com/help/contact/305593649477238 to display Facebook's Memorialization Request page.

(2) Enter the full name of your loved one into the Full Name of Deceased Person box.

(1)

Memorialization Request

Please use this form to request the memorialization of a deceased person's account. We extend our condolences and appreciate your patience and understanding throughout this process. Note: Under penalty of perjury, this form is solely for reporting a deceased person's timeline to be memorialized.

Full name of deceased person
As it's listed on the account

(2)

3 Enter the URL of the deceased person's Timeline into the Link to the Timeline You'd Like to Report box.

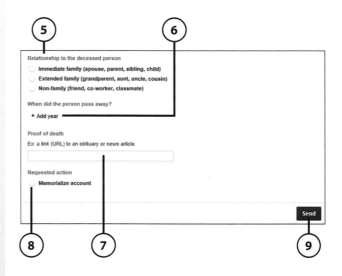

Timeline URL

You can find the URL of the person's Timeline page by opening that page in your web browser and copying the address that appears in your browser's address box.

4 Enter any of the email addresses used by this person into the Email Addresses Listed on the Account box.

5 Go to the Relationship to Deceased Person section and check how you're related—Immediate Family, Extended Family, or Non-Family.

6 In the When Did This Person Pass Away? section, click the Add Year, Add Month, and Add Date links to enter the person's date of death.

7 Enter a link to any online article or website reporting this person's death into the Proof of Death box. You can link to this person's online obituary or memorial page from the attending funeral home.

8 Check the Memorialize Account option.

9 Click the Send button.

It's Not All Good

Mistaken Memorialization

What do you do if someone memorializes your account—either on purpose or by mistake—and you're not dead yet? You need to contact Facebook via a special form to say you're still alive and want to continue using your account. You won't be able to log into Facebook if your account is in a memorialized state, so go to www.facebook.com/help/contact/292558237463098 and fill out the form there.

Remove an Account

If you'd rather not have a loved one's Facebook account memorialized, you can ask Facebook to remove the person's account from the site. Believe it or not, this is a more involved process than memorializing the account.

In preparation for this process, you need some proof of the person's death, typically a copy of the death certificate. This documentation needs to be scanned into your computer as an image file that you can upload to Facebook when required.

(1) From your web browser, go to www.facebook.com/help/contact/?id=228813257197480 to display the Special Request for Deceased Person's Account page.

(2) Enter your name into the Your Full Name box.

(3) Enter the name of the deceased person into the Full Name on the Deceased Person's Account box.

(2) **(1)**

Special Request for Deceased Person's Account

Please use this form to request the removal of a deceased person's account or for memorialization special requests. We extend our condolences and appreciate your patience and understanding throughout this process. Unrelated inquires received through this channel may not receive a response. To protect the privacy of people on Facebook, we cannot provide anyone with login information for accounts.

Your full name

Full name on the deceased person's account

Account email address of the deceased person
The email that may have been used to create the account

Web address (URL) of the timeline
https://www.facebook.com/...

(3)

4. Enter the email address used by the deceased person (if you know it) into the Account Email Address of the Deceased Person box.

5. Enter the URL of the deceased person's Timeline page into the Web Address (URL) of the Timeline box.

6. Go to the Relationship to the Person section and check how you're related—Immediate Family, Extended Family, or Non-Family.

7. Go to the How Can We Help You? section and select the Please Remove This Account option.

8. In the When Did This Person Pass Away? section, provide the deceased user's date of death.

9. Go to the Please Provide Verification That You're an Immediate Family Member section and click the Browse button to select the file for the death certificate or other document.

10. When you return to the Special Request for Deceased Person's Account page, enter any additional comments or requests into the Additional Information box.

11. Click the Send button.

Special Request for Deceased Person's Account

Please use this form to request the removal of a deceased person's account or for memorialization special requests. We extend our condolences and appreciate your patience and understanding throughout this process. Unrelated inquires received through this channel may not receive a response. To protect the privacy of people on Facebook, we cannot provide anyone with login information for accounts.

Your full name

Full name on the deceased person's account

Account email address of the deceased person
The email that may have been used to create the account

Web address (URL) of the timeline
https://www.facebook.com/...

Relationship to the person
○ Immediate family (spouse, parent, sibling, child)
○ Extended family (grandparent, aunt, uncle, cousin)
○ Non-family (friend, co-worker, classmate)

How can we help you?
○ Please memorialize this account
○ Please remove this account
○ I have a special request
○ I have a question

When did the person pass away?
+ Add year

Please provide verification that you're an immediate family member
You'll need to upload documentation like a death certificate, the deceased person's birth certificate, or proof of authority
[Browse...]

Additional information
If you have a special request or question, please use this space to provide more information

[Send]

Download Content from a Deceased Person's Account

Most Facebook users put a large chunk of their lives online, in the form of photos, videos, and such. Rather than abandon those photos and other content when a loved one dies, you can ask to download that content for your own use.

Due to privacy concerns, which continue after a person's death, this process is somewhat involved. You need to have a copy of your driver's license or other government-issued ID scanned into your computer to upload to Facebook when asked; you also need to scan a copy of the deceased person's death certificate.

1. From your web browser, go to www.facebook.com/help/contact/398036060275245 to display the Requesting Content From a Deceased Person's Account page.

2. Check Yes that you're an authorized representative of the deceased person. The page expands.

3. If the person is a minor, check Yes. Otherwise, check No. The page expands.

4. When you're asked if you have a will or power of attorney that specifically addressed this person's Facebook account, click Yes if you do and No if you don't.

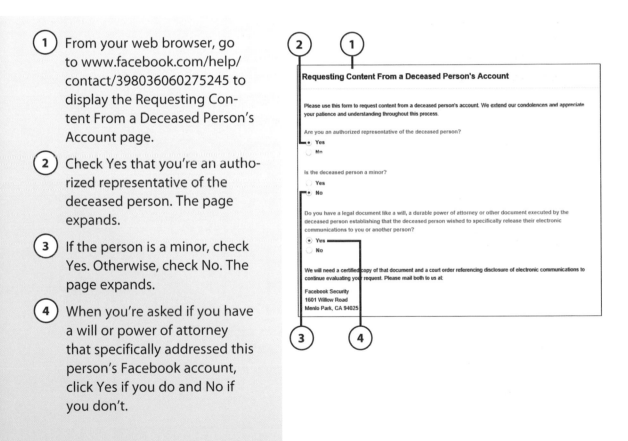

Requesting Content From a Deceased Person's Account

Please use this form to request content from a deceased person's account. We extend our condolences and appreciate your patience and understanding throughout this process.

Are you an authorized representative of the deceased person?
- ● Yes
- ○ No

Is the deceased person a minor?
- ○ Yes
- ● No

Do you have a legal document like a will, a durable power of attorney or other document executed by the deceased person establishing that the deceased person wished to specifically release their electronic communications to you or another person?
- ● Yes
- ○ No

We will need a certified copy of that document and a court order referencing disclosure of electronic communications to continue evaluating your request. Please mail both to us at:

Facebook Security
1601 Willow Road
Menlo Park, CA 94025

(5) If you checked Yes, send a certified copy of that document and a court order referencing the disclosure of this and other electronic content to the following address:

Facebook Security
1601 Willow Road
Menlo Park, CA 94025

(6) If you checked no, check to accept the disclaimer.

(7) Enter your name into the Your Full Name box.

(8) Enter your street address into the Your Mailing Address box.

(9) Enter your email address into the Your Email Address box.

(10) In the Any Documents Establishing Your Connection to the Deceased Person section, click the Browse button and select the file(s) required.

(11) In the Copy of the Deceased Person's Death Certificate section, click the Browse button and select the file for the scanned-in death certificate.

(12) Click the Send button. Facebook now evaluates your request and will eventually respond with further instructions.

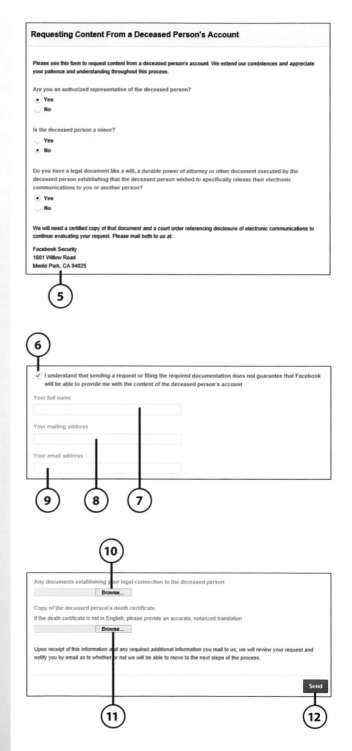

It's Not All Good

Incapacitated Users

The situation is less clear if you're still alive but incapacitated, without the ability to sign onto Facebook on your own behalf. At present, Facebook offers no formal process for a spouse or other family member to access an incapacitated user's account. The best thing to do, if you can, is have the person give you his password, and then log onto his account yourself, on his behalf. You can then delete or deactivate the account, as per the incapacitated user's request.

If your loved one is unable to provide you with his Facebook password, the situation is much more murky. You can try contacting Facebook on the behalf of your loved one, but it's unclear whether Facebook has the right to let you access that person's account. But it's worth trying.

To contact Facebook about this or other issues, email info@facebook.com or call 800-608-1600.

Facebook
on the iPhone

Facebook on an
Android device

Facebook
on the iPad

In this chapter, you find out how to use Facebook on your smartphone or tablet.

Using Facebook on Your iPhone, iPad, or Android Device

More and more of us are using our phones and tablets to access the Internet. It's convenient to check in on the web while we're on the go.

For that reason, Facebook has developed mobile apps for the iPhone, iPad, and Android devices. You don't have to wait until you get home to check your Facebook News Feed—or post a status update or photo!

Using Facebook on an iPhone

If you're an iPhone user, there's a Facebook app that lets you do pretty much everything you do on your computer on your phone, instead. You can find the Facebook app in Apple's iPhone App Store; just search the store for "Facebook" and download the app—it's free.

Logging In

The first time you launch any Facebook mobile app, you need to enter your email address and password to log in.

Navigate Facebook's iPhone App

When you first open Facebook's iPhone app you see the News Feed screen. This is a good starting place for all your Facebook-related activity.

1. Tap the News Feed icon at any time to display the News Feed screen.

2. Swipe up to scroll down the screen and view older posts.

3. Refresh the News Feed by pulling down from the top of the screen.

4. Tap Status to post a status update.

5. Post a photo by tapping Photo.

6. Tap Check In to "check in" (post your location only).

It's Not All Good

Beware Stalkers

Using the Check In feature to broadcast your current location can alert any potential stalkers where to find you—or tell potential burglars that your house is currently empty. Because of the potential dangers, think twice about using this feature.

(7) Tap the Requests icon to view and respond to friend requests.

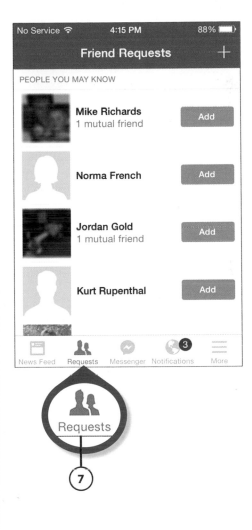

(8) Tap the Notifications icon to view notifications from Facebook.

(9) Tap the More icon to view your favorite pages and groups.

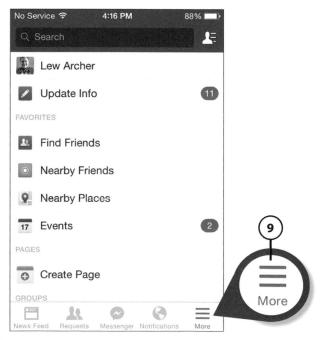

Read and Respond to Posts

Reading and responding to posts with Facebook's iPhone app is similar to doing so on your computer.

(1) Tap the Like icon to like a post.

(2) Tap the Comment icon to comment on a post.

(3) Tap the Share icon to share a post.

(4) Tap the poster's name to view that person's Timeline page.

(5) If the post includes a photo, tap the photo to view it full screen.

(6) If the post includes a link to another web page, tap the link or thumbnail to view that page on a new screen.

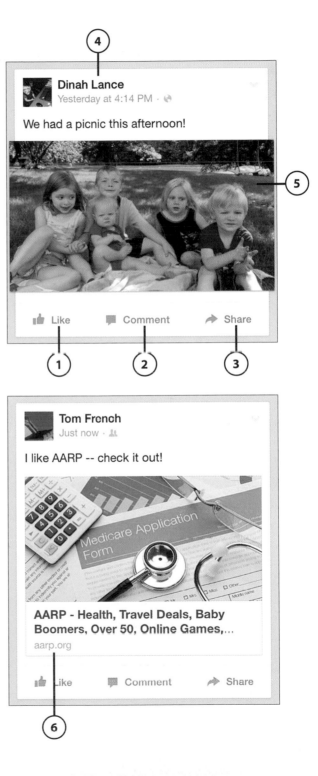

Post Status Updates

(1) Tap the Status icon to display the Update Status screen.

(2) Type the text of your message into the What's On Your Mind? area.

(3) Tap the Camera icon to include a photo or video with your post.

(4) Tap the Tag Friends icon to tag another person in your post.

(5) Tap the What Are You Doing? icon to tell others what you're doing.

(6) Tap the Add Location icon to include your location in the post.

(7) Tap the Privacy icon in the To: section to change who can see the post.

(8) Tap Post to post the status update.

☑ Status   ◉ Photo   ◉ Check In

(1)

(7)

No Service 📶	4:19 PM	⬆ 88% 🔋
Cancel	**Update Status**	Post

To: 🌐 Public   >

What's on your mind?

(8)

(2)

(4)   (5)

(3) 📷   👤   😊   📍   (6)

Q W E R T Y U I O P

A S D F G H J K L

⬆ Z X C V B N M ⌫

.?123   space   return

>>>*Go Further*
CAMERA APP

Apple also lets you post pictures to Facebook directly from your iPhone's built-in Camera app. After you take a photo, tap the Share button, and then tap the Facebook icon. When the Update Status screen appears, add a message and complete the status update as normal to post the photo to your Facebook feed.

Using Facebook on an iPad

Facebook looks a little different on the bigger iPad screen than it does on the iPhone. It still does all the same things but with a slightly different layout.

Navigate Facebook's iPad App

When you first open the Facebook app, you see the News Feed screen. This screen looks different depending on how you're holding your iPad.

1 In landscape mode (held horizontally), you see the News Feed on the left with a Favorites panel on the right side of the screen. Swipe up to scroll down the screen and view older posts.

News Feed

Favorites panel

2 In portrait mode (held vertically), you see the normal News Feed with no additional sidebars. Tap the three-bar icon at the top-left corner of the screen to display the navigation sidebar.

3 Refresh the News Feed by pulling down from the top of the screen.

4 Tap Status to post a status update.

5 Tap Photo to post a photo.

6 Tap Check In to "check in" (post your location only).

7 Tap the Requests icon to view and respond to friend requests.

8 Tap the Notifications icon to view notifications from Facebook.

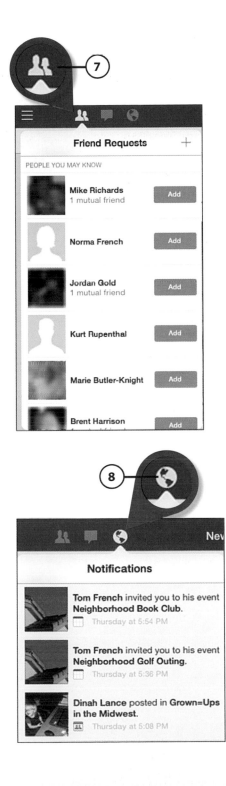

Read and Respond to Posts

Reading and responding to posts with Facebook's iPad app is similar to doing so with the iPhone app.

(1) Tap the Like icon to like a post.

(2) Tap the Comment icon to comment on a post.

(3) Tap the Share icon to share a post.

(4) Tap the poster's name to view that person's Timeline page.

(5) If the post includes a photo, tap the photo to view it full screen.

(6) If the post includes a link to another web page, tap the link or thumbnail to view that page on a new screen.

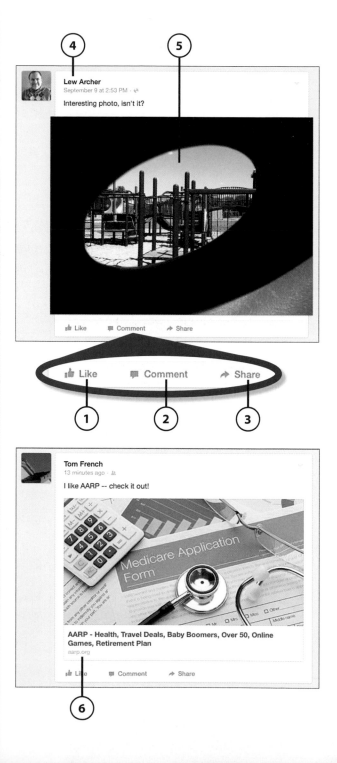

Post Status Updates

You post new status updates from the News Feed screen.

1. Tap the Status icon to display the Update Status screen.

2. Type the text of your message into the What's On Your Mind? area.

3. Tap the Camera icon to include a photo or video with your post.

4. Tap the Tag Friends icon to tag another person in your post.

5. Tap the What Are You Doing? icon to tell others what you're doing.

6. Tap the Add Location icon to include your location in the post.

7. Tap the Privacy icon to change who can see the post.

8. Tap Post to post the status update.

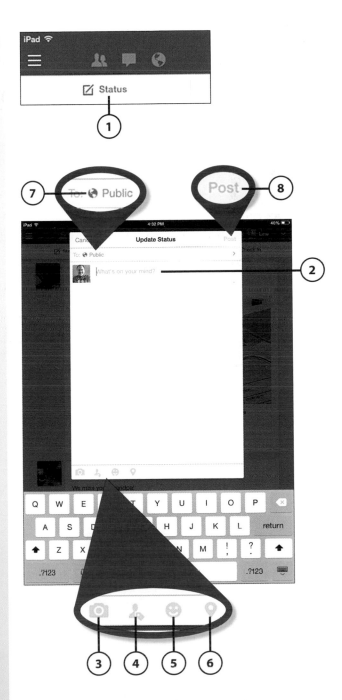

Using Facebook on an Android Device

If you use an Android phone or tablet, Facebook has a mobile app for you, too. You can find Facebook's Android app in the Google Play Store; just search the store for "Facebook" and download the app—it's free.

>>>*Go Further*
REALPAD TABLET

AARP offers the RealPad, an Android tablet designed with tech-shy people in mind. The RealPad is a 7.85-inch tablet pre-loaded with a number of popular apps and helpful how-to videos. It comes with free 24/7 customer service support and a free one-year membership to AARP, and sells for $189. As an Android tablet, it runs Facebook's Android app, described here. Learn more at www.aarprealpad.org.

Navigate Facebook's Android App

The Facebook app for Android looks a lot like the Facebook app for iPhone. As with the iPhone version, when you launch the Android app you see the News Feed screen.

1. Tap the News Feed icon to return to the News Feed at any time.

2. Swipe up to scroll down the screen and view older posts.

3. Refresh the News Feed by pulling down from the top of the screen and then releasing.

4. Tap Status to post a status update.

5 Tap Photo to post a photo.

6 Tap Check in to "check in" to a given location.

7 Tap the Friend Requests icon or scroll right from the News Feed screen to view friend requests.

8 Tap the Notifications icon or scroll right from the previous screen to view Facebook notifications.

9 Tap the More icon or scroll right from the Notifications screen to view your favorite pages and groups.

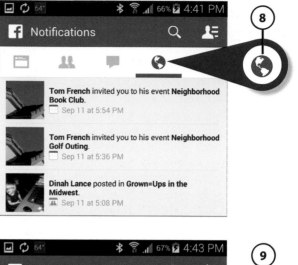

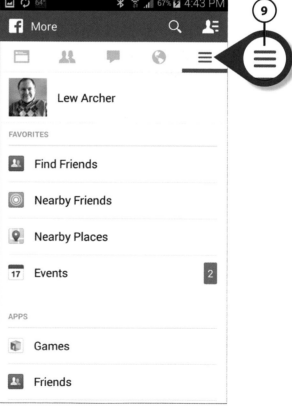

Read and Respond to Posts

You read and respond to posts from your friends on the News Feed screen.

 Tap the Like icon to like a post.

2 Tap the Comment icon to comment on a post.

3 Tap the Share icon to share a post.

4 Tap the poster's name to view that person's Timeline page.

5 If the post includes a photo, tap the photo to view it full screen.

6 If the post includes a link to another web page, tap the link or thumbnail to view that page on a new screen.

Post a Status Update

You create new status updates from the app's News Feed screen.

(1) Tap the Status icon to display the Write Post screen.

(2) Type the text of your message into the What's On Your Mind? area.

(3) Tap the Camera icon to include a photo or video with your post.

(4) Tap the Tag Friends icon to tag another person in your post.

(5) Tap the What Are You Doing? icon to tell others what you're doing.

(6) Tap the Add Location icon to include your location in the post.

(7) Tap the Privacy icon in the To: section to change who can see the post.

(8) Tap Post to post the status update.

Using the Facebook Messenger App

If you want to chat with a Facebook friend in real time, you can't do it from the Facebook mobile app. Instead, you need to use a separate app, called Facebook Messenger, to do this sort of instant messaging. Like the regular Facebook app, the Messenger app is free for downloading for both Apple and Android devices.

The Facebook Messenger app does more than just connect you with your Facebook friends, however. If you opt for the default installation, the Messenger app taps into your phone's contacts list and identifies those contacts who are also on Facebook. This means that you can instant message with any of your contacts who are also Facebook users, even if they're not currently on your friends list.

Note that the Messenger app looks a little different on Android devices than it does on your iPhone or iPad. We're showing the iPhone version of this app for our examples, but the same functionality exists on the Android version—some of the icons are just in different places.

Send and Receive Text Messages

Just like the Facebook website does, Messenger enables you to send and receive either real-time text messages or private email-like messages. If the person you want to talk to is online, you communicate in real-time text chat. If the person you want to talk to is not currently online, you send that person a private text message instead.

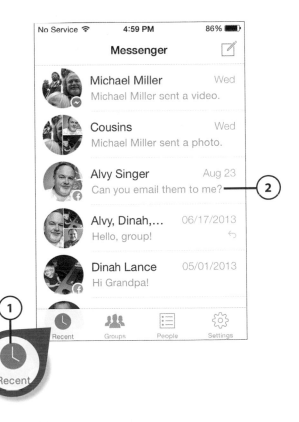

1. Tap the Recent icon to view a list of your most recent text conversations and private messages.

2. Tap a conversation header to view messages between you and that person.

(3) To continue the conversation, use your phone's onscreen keyboard to type a message into the Type a Message box.

(4) Tap Send to send the message to the other person.

(5) Create a new text message by tapping the New Message icon to open the New Message screen.

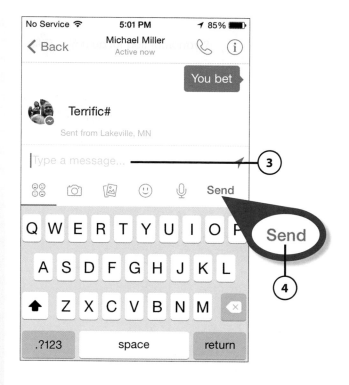

>>>Go Further

MESSAGING FROM THE PEOPLE SCREEN

You can also send messages directly from Messenger's People screen. Tap the People icon to display a list of your Facebook friends who are using the Messenger app and tap a person's name to start the conversation.

6 All your friends and contacts are listed on this screen. Those currently online and available for real-time messaging have a blue icon next to their picture. Tap a person's name or picture to begin the conversation.

7 Enter your message into the Type a Message box.

8 To insert an emoji (emoticon—like a smiley face) in your message, tap the Emoji icon, and then tap the desired item. To switch back to text entry, tap the Text icon. (The icon toggles between Text and Emoji mode.)

9 Tap the Send icon to send the message.

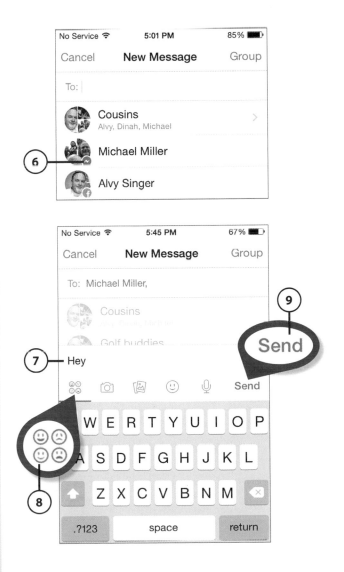

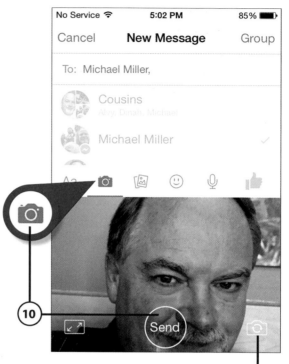

10 Tap the Camera icon to take a photo and send it to your friend. The bottom of the screen turns into a photo viewfinder with your phone's front-facing camera activated. (To switch to the normal camera, tap the Switch View icon.) Aim properly then tap the Send button.

Switch View icon

>>>Go Further
SENDING VIDEOS

On the Android version of the Messenger app, you can also send videos to your friends. Tap and hold the Send button to shoot a video; release the button to send the video.

(11) To send a photo from your
phone's photo gallery, tap the
Photo icon and select the photo
from the gallery displayed at the
bottom of the screen.

(12) Send a "sticker" (kind of a large
emoji) by tapping the Sticker
button, and then select an item.

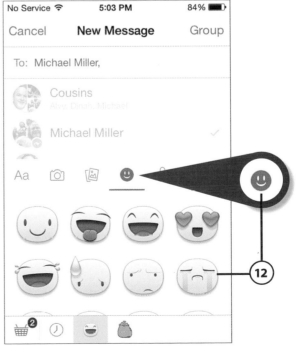

13 Send a voice message by tapping the Microphone icon then tapping and holding the Record button. Start speaking and release the button when you're done.

14 Tap the Like button to give your friend a thumb's up.

>>>Go Further

PHONE CALLS

If the person you're messaging with is in your phone's contacts list, or if that person's phone number is listed with Facebook, you can turn your text message into a phone call. From within any conversation, tap the telephone icon to place the call.

Create a Group Conversation

The Messenger app isn't just for one-on-one conversations. You can also participate in group chats.

1. Tap the Groups icon to display the Groups page.

2. Tap Create to open the New Group screen.

3. Enter a name for your group.

4. Tap the names of people you want to include in this group.

5. Tap Create.

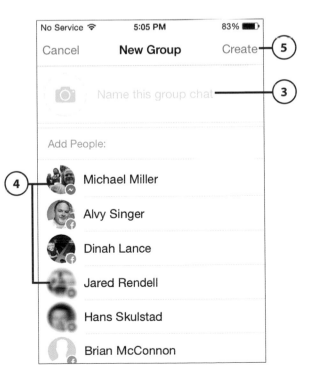

6 The new group now appears on the Groups page. Tap the group to open that group's conversation page.

7 Enter message text into the Type a Message box.

8 Tap the Send icon to send the message. Your message and messages from other group members appear in the center of the screen.

9 Tap any of the other icons to send to the group an emoji, photo, sticker, or voice message.

Using Facebook's Paper App

If you use an iPhone, Facebook has an alternate app you can use in place of its normal mobile app. This app, dubbed Paper, functions as both a Facebook app and a news reader. It also incorporates the messaging function now absent from the main mobile app. It's available for free from the Apple App Store—but it's not currently available for the iPad or for Android devices.

Navigate the Paper App

You navigate the Paper app primarily by swiping—up, down, left, and right.

(1) When you launch the Paper app, you see posts from your News Feed in tall "cards" along the bottom of the screen. To view additional posts, scroll horizontally; the newest stories pop up at the left, and you scroll right to read older stories.

(2) Above the news feed is an automatically scrolling list of featured stories. These are typically the most popular (and most recent) posts from your Facebook friends and groups. Each featured story appears by itself on the full top-screen space; the image from the story fills the space, while the initial text is superimposed on top. Tap a featured story to read it full screen.

3 To view non-Facebook content, swipe the featured post to the left. Keep swiping to the left to view additional "sections," which are organized by topic (Headlines, Pop Life, Home, and the like). Content in these sections comes from all across the web as well as from Facebook groups and users.

4 Tap the Friends Requests icon to display and respond to Facebook friend requests.

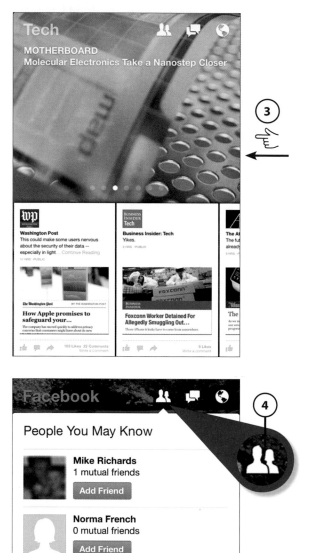

5 Tap the Messages icon to read and send private messages to other users.

6 Tap the Notifications icon to view Facebook notifications.

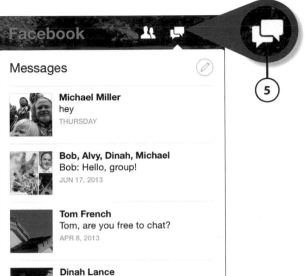

Facebook

Messages

Michael Miller
hey
THURSDAY

Bob, Alvy, Dinah, Michael
Bob: Hello, group!
JUN 17, 2013

Tom French
Tom, are you free to chat?
APR 8, 2013

Dinah Lance
Bye
FEB 8, 2013

Bob, Michael
Lew: Here's a photo of my
grandson Collin.

5

Facebook

Notifications

Tom French invited you to his
event Neighborhood Book Club.
THURSDAY

Tom French invited you to his
event Neighborhood Golf Outing.
THURSDAY

Dinah Lance posted in
Grown=Ups in the Midwest.
THURSDAY

Events

Neighborhood Golf Outing
October 4 at 9:00 AM
Brookshire Golf Course
YOU'RE INVITED

6

Read Posts

Posts from your News Feed are easier to read on the Paper app—in part because you can display each post full screen.

(1) To view an entire post, tap or drag the story up from the bottom (or down from the top) to fill the entire screen. You can then side scroll from one full-screen story to the next.

(2) Tap Like to like a post.

(3) Tap Comment to comment on a post.

(4) Tap Share to share a post.

(5) To view the next post, swipe the current post to the left.

(6) To view the previous post, swipe the current post to the right.

(7) To return to the News Feed, tap or drag downward in an open post.

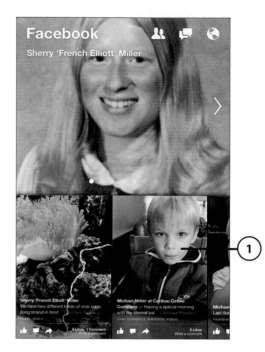

Create a New Post

You can also use the Paper app to post status updates to Facebook.

(1) Swipe down from the top of the main screen to display the menu screen

(2) Tap Create Post.

3 When the next screen appears, start typing into the Write Something area.

4 Tap the icon at the bottom left of this screen to add a photo to your post.

5 Tap Post when you're done.

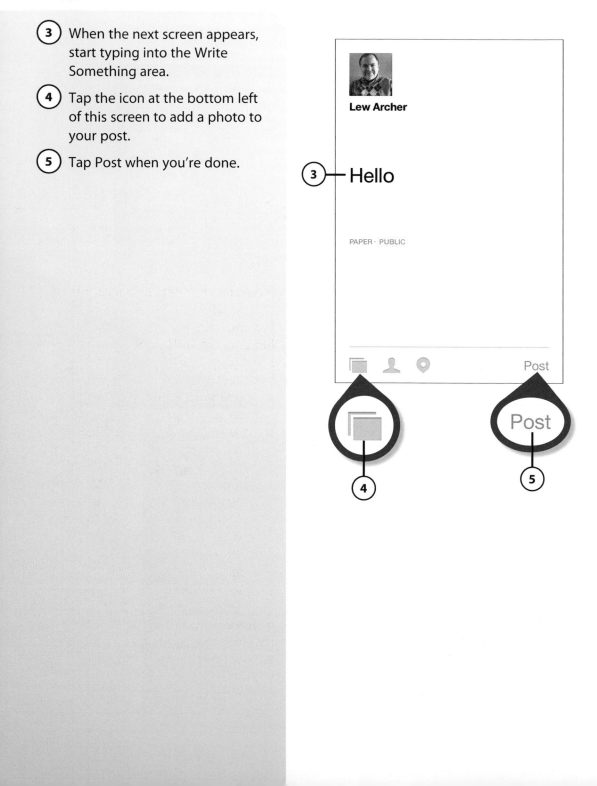

Index

Symbols

REGISTER THIS PRODUCT
SAVE 35%*
ON YOUR NEXT PURCHASE!

How to Register Your Product

- Go to quepublishing.com/register
- Sign in or create an account
- Enter the 10- or 13-digit ISBN that appears on the back cover of your product

Benefits of Registering

- Ability to download product updates
- Access to bonus chapters and workshop files
- A 35% coupon to be used on your next purchase – valid for 30 days
  > To obtain your coupon, click on "Manage Codes" in the right column of your Account page
- Receive special offers on new editions and related Que products

Please note that the benefits for registering may vary by product. Benefits will be listed on your Account page under Registered Products.

We value and respect your privacy. Your email address will not be sold to any third party company.

* 35% discount code presented after product registration is valid on most print books, eBooks, and full-course videos sold on QuePublishing.com. Discount may not be combined with any other offer and is not redeemable for cash. Discount code expires after 30 days from the time of product registration. Offer subject to change.

quepublishing.com